Hi there!

I'M LYNSEY AND I'M SO EXCITED TO SHARE THIS TWIN TRACKER WITH YOU.

First of all... CONGRATULATIONS!

I remember the weeks following that very first ultrasound that revealed there were not one, but THREE babies growing in me. I felt overwhelmed, emotional, terrified, anxious, confused about how we were going to get through it. To be honest, it took a little while for feelings of excitement to come around.

I researched everything under the sun, but ultimately gained some of the very best knowledge from parents who had blazed the trail of rearing multiples ahead of me. I started working on resources for other parents to help them become confident in their pregnancy and not just survive - but set them up to THRIVE - in the chaos of that first year.

I hope you find this guide to be a valuable tool in tracking breast or bottle feedings, sleep, diapers, meds & anything else you need to make note of.

Twin Tracker helps you coordinate more effectively when there are multiple caretakers and to make life as a busy parent of twins much easier.

Let's do this!

-Lynsey

To Do

Reminders

Baby B

Time	Breast/Bottle	Diaper	Meds
am pm	oz./R min. L		
am pm	oz./R min. L		
am pm	oz./R min. L		
am pm	oz./R min. L		
am pm	oz./R min. L		
am pm	oz./R min. L		
am pm	oz./R min. L		
am pm	oz./R min. L		

Naps

start	finish

Notes

Baby A

Time	Breast/Bottle	Diaper	Meds
am pm	oz./R min. L		
am pm	oz./R min. L		
am pm	oz./R min. L		
am pm	oz./R min. L		
am pm	oz./R min. L		
am pm	oz./R min. L		
am pm	oz./R min. L		
am pm	oz./R min. L		

Naps

start	finish

Notes

twin tracker

TODAY IS:

twin tracker

To Do

Reminders

Baby A

Time		Breast/Bottle	Diaper	Meds
am	pm	oz. / R min. L		
am	pm	oz. / R min. L		
am	pm	oz. / R min. L		
am	pm	oz. / R min. L		
am	pm	oz. / R min. L		
am	pm	oz. / R min. L		
am	pm	oz. / R min. L		
am	pm	oz. / R min. L		

Naps

start	finish

Notes

Baby B

Time		Breast/Bottle	Diaper	Meds
am	pm	oz. / R min. L		
am	pm	oz. / R min. L		
am	pm	oz. / R min. L		
am	pm	oz. / R min. L		
am	pm	oz. / R min. L		
am	pm	oz. / R min. L		
am	pm	oz. / R min. L		
am	pm	oz. / R min. L		

Naps

start	finish

Notes

TODAY IS:

twin tracker

To Do

Reminders

Baby A

Time	Breast/Bottle	Diaper	Meds
am pm	oz./R min. L		
am pm	oz./R min. L		
am pm	oz./R min. L		
am pm	oz./R min. L		
am pm	oz./R min. L		
am pm	oz./R min. L		
am pm	oz./R min. L		
am pm	oz./R min. L		

Naps

start	finish

Notes

Baby B

Time	Breast/Bottle	Diaper	Meds
am pm	oz./R min. L		
am pm	oz./R min. L		
am pm	oz./R min. L		
am pm	oz./R min. L		
am pm	oz./R min. L		
am pm	oz./R min. L		
am pm	oz./R min. L		
am pm	oz./R min. L		

Naps

start	finish

Notes

TODAY IS:

twin tracker

To Do

Reminders

Baby B

Time	Breast/Bottle	Diaper	Meds
am pm	oz. / R min. L		
am pm	oz. / R min. L		
am pm	oz. / R min. L		
am pm	oz. / R min. L		
am pm	oz. / R min. L		
am pm	oz. / R min. L		
am pm	oz. / R min. L		

Baby A

Time	Breast/Bottle	Diaper	Meds
am pm	oz. / R min. L		
am pm	oz. / R min. L		
am pm	oz. / R min. L		
am pm	oz. / R min. L		
am pm	oz. / R min. L		
am pm	oz. / R min. L		
am pm	oz. / R min. L		

Naps

start	finish

Notes

Naps

start	finish

Notes

TODAY IS:

To Do

Reminders

Baby B

Time	Breast/Bottle		Diaper	Meds
am pm	oz./R	min. L		
am pm	oz./R	min. L		
am pm	oz./R	min. L		
am pm	oz./R	min. L		
am pm	oz./R	min. L		
am pm	oz./R	min. L		
am pm	oz./R	min. L		
am pm	oz./R	min. L		

Naps
start		finish

Notes

Baby A

Time	Breast/Bottle		Diaper	Meds
am pm	oz./R	min. L		
am pm	oz./R	min. L		
am pm	oz./R	min. L		
am pm	oz./R	min. L		
am pm	oz./R	min. L		
am pm	oz./R	min. L		
am pm	oz./R	min. L		
am pm	oz./R	min. L		

Naps
start		finish

Notes

TODAY IS:

twin tracker

twin tracker

Baby A

Time	Breast/Bottle		Diaper	Meds
am pm	oz./R min. L			
am pm	oz./R min. L			
am pm	oz./R min. L			
am pm	oz./R min. L			
am pm	oz./R min. L			
am pm	oz./R min. L			
am pm	oz./R min. L			
am pm	oz./R min. L			

Naps

start	finish

Notes

Baby B

Time	Breast/Bottle		Diaper	Meds
am pm	oz./R min. L			
am pm	oz./R min. L			
am pm	oz./R min. L			
am pm	oz./R min. L			
am pm	oz./R min. L			
am pm	oz./R min. L			
am pm	oz./R min. L			
am pm	oz./R min. L			

Naps

start	finish

Notes

To Do

Reminders

TODAY IS:

To Do

Reminders

Baby B

Time	Breast/Bottle		Diaper	Meds
	oz./R	min. L		
am / pm				
am / pm				
am / pm				
am / pm				
am / pm				
am / pm				
am / pm				
am / pm				

Naps

start		finish

Notes

Baby A

Time	Breast/Bottle		Diaper	Meds
	oz./R	min. L		
am / pm				
am / pm				
am / pm				
am / pm				
am / pm				
am / pm				
am / pm				
am / pm				

Naps

start		finish

Notes

TODAY IS:

twin tracker

twin tracker

To Do

Reminders

Baby B

Time	Breast/Bottle		Diaper	Meds
am pm	oz./R	min. L		
am pm	oz./R	min. L		
am pm	oz./R	min. L		
am pm	oz./R	min. L		
am pm	oz./R	min. L		
am pm	oz./R	min. L		
am pm	oz./R	min. L		
am pm	oz./R	min. L		

Naps

start	finish

Notes

Baby A

Time	Breast/Bottle		Diaper	Meds
am pm	oz./R	min. L		
am pm	oz./R	min. L		
am pm	oz./R	min. L		
am pm	oz./R	min. L		
am pm	oz./R	min. L		
am pm	oz./R	min. L		
am pm	oz./R	min. L		
am pm	oz./R	min. L		

Naps

start	finish

Notes

TODAY IS:

twin tracker

To Do

Reminders

Baby A

Time	Breast/Bottle		Diaper	Meds
am pm	oz./R	min. L		
am pm	oz./R	min. L		
am pm	oz./R	min. L		
am pm	oz./R	min. L		
am pm	oz./R	min. L		
am pm	oz./R	min. L		
am pm	oz./R	min. L		
am pm	oz./R	min. L		

Naps
start	finish

Notes

Baby B

Time	Breast/Bottle		Diaper	Meds
am pm	oz./R	min. L		
am pm	oz./R	min. L		
am pm	oz./R	min. L		
am pm	oz./R	min. L		
am pm	oz./R	min. L		
am pm	oz./R	min. L		
am pm	oz./R	min. L		
am pm	oz./R	min. L		

Naps
start	finish

Notes

TODAY IS:

To Do

Reminders

Baby B

Time		Breast/Bottle	Diaper	Meds
am pm		oz./R min. L		
am pm		oz./R min. L		
am pm		oz./R min. L		
am pm		oz./R min. L		
am pm		oz./R min. L		
am pm		oz./R min. L		
am pm		oz./R min. L		
am pm		oz./R min. L		

Naps

start	finish

Notes

Baby A

Time		Breast/Bottle	Diaper	Meds
am pm		oz./R min. L		
am pm		oz./R min. L		
am pm		oz./R min. L		
am pm		oz./R min. L		
am pm		oz./R min. L		
am pm		oz./R min. L		
am pm		oz./R min. L		
am pm		oz./R min. L		

Naps

start	finish

Notes

twin tracker

TODAY IS:

twin tracker

To Do

Reminders

Baby A

Time	Breast/Bottle	Diaper	Meds
am pm	oz./R min. L		
am pm	oz./R min. L		
am pm	oz./R min. L		
am pm	oz./R min. L		
am pm	oz./R min. L		
am pm	oz./R min. L		
am pm	oz./R min. L		

Naps

start			finish	

Notes

Baby B

Time	Breast/Bottle	Diaper	Meds
am pm	oz./R min. L		
am pm	oz./R min. L		
am pm	oz./R min. L		
am pm	oz./R min. L		
am pm	oz./R min. L		
am pm	oz./R min. L		
am pm	oz./R min. L		
am pm	oz./R min. L		

Naps

start			finish	

Notes

TODAY IS:

twin tracker

To Do

Baby A

Time	Breast/Bottle		Diaper	Meds
	oz./R	min. L		
am pm				
am pm				
am pm				
am pm				
am pm				
am pm				
am pm				
am pm				

Naps
start	finish

Notes

Baby B

Time	Breast/Bottle		Diaper	Meds
	oz./R	min. L		
am pm				
am pm				
am pm				
am pm				
am pm				
am pm				
am pm				
am pm				

Naps
start	finish

Notes

Reminders

TODAY IS:

twin tracker

To Do

Reminders

Baby B

Time	Breast/Bottle	Diaper	Meds
am pm	oz./R min. L		
am pm	oz./R min. L		
am pm	oz./R min. L		
am pm	oz./R min. L		
am pm	oz./R min. L		
am pm	oz./R min. L		
am pm	oz./R min. L		
am pm	oz./R min. L		

Naps

start	finish

Notes

Baby A

Time	Breast/Bottle	Diaper	Meds
am pm	oz./R min. L		
am pm	oz./R min. L		
am pm	oz./R min. L		
am pm	oz./R min. L		
am pm	oz./R min. L		
am pm	oz./R min. L		
am pm	oz./R min. L		
am pm	oz./R min. L		

Naps

start	finish

Notes

TODAY IS:

twin tracker

To Do

Baby B

Time	Breast/Bottle		Diaper	Meds
am pm	oz. / R min. L			
am pm	oz. / R min. L			
am pm	oz. / R min. L			
am pm	oz. / R min. L			
am pm	oz. / R min. L			
am pm	oz. / R min. L			
am pm	oz. / R min. L			
am pm	oz. / R min. L			

Baby A

Time	Breast/Bottle		Diaper	Meds
am pm	oz. / R min. L			
am pm	oz. / R min. L			
am pm	oz. / R min. L			
am pm	oz. / R min. L			
am pm	oz. / R min. L			
am pm	oz. / R min. L			
am pm	oz. / R min. L			
am pm	oz. / R min. L			

Reminders

Notes

Naps

start	finish

Notes

Naps

start	finish

TODAY IS:

twin tracker

To Do

Reminders

Baby A

Time	Breast/Bottle	Diaper	Meds
am pm	oz. / R min. L		
am pm	oz. / R min. L		
am pm	oz. / R min. L		
am pm	oz. / R min. L		
am pm	oz. / R min. L		
am pm	oz. / R min. L		
am pm	oz. / R min. L		
am pm	oz. / R min. L		

Naps

start	finish

Notes

Baby B

Time	Breast/Bottle	Diaper	Meds
am pm	oz. / R min. L		
am pm	oz. / R min. L		
am pm	oz. / R min. L		
am pm	oz. / R min. L		
am pm	oz. / R min. L		
am pm	oz. / R min. L		
am pm	oz. / R min. L		
am pm	oz. / R min. L		

Naps

start	finish

Notes

TODAY IS:

twin tracker

To Do

Baby B

Time	Breast/Bottle		Diaper	Meds
am pm	oz./R min. L			
am pm	oz./R min. L			
am pm	oz./R min. L			
am pm	oz./R min. L			
am pm	oz./R min. L			
am pm	oz./R min. L			
am pm	oz./R min. L			
am pm	oz./R min. L			

Naps
start	finish

Notes

Baby A

Time	Breast/Bottle		Diaper	Meds
am pm	oz./R min. L			
am pm	oz./R min. L			
am pm	oz./R min. L			
am pm	oz./R min. L			
am pm	oz./R min. L			
am pm	oz./R min. L			
am pm	oz./R min. L			
am pm	oz./R min. L			

Naps
start	finish

Notes

Reminders

TODAY IS:

twin tracker

To Do

Reminders

Baby B

Time	Breast/Bottle	Diaper	Meds
am pm	oz. / R min. L		
am pm	oz. / R min. L		
am pm	oz. / R min. L		
am pm	oz. / R min. L		
am pm	oz. / R min. L		
am pm	oz. / R min. L		
am pm	oz. / R min. L		
am pm	oz. / R min. L		

Notes

Naps

start	finish

Baby A

Time	Breast/Bottle	Diaper	Meds
am pm	oz. / R min. L		
am pm	oz. / R min. L		
am pm	oz. / R min. L		
am pm	oz. / R min. L		
am pm	oz. / R min. L		
am pm	oz. / R min. L		
am pm	oz. / R min. L		
am pm	oz. / R min. L		

Notes

Naps

start	finish

TODAY IS:

To Do

© 2022 LYNSEY WEST | ALL RIGHTS RESERVED

Reminders

Baby B

Time	Breast/Bottle	Diaper	Meds
am pm	oz./ R min. L		
am pm	oz./ R min. L		
am pm	oz./ R min. L		
am pm	oz./ R min. L		
am pm	oz./ R min. L		
am pm	oz./ R min. L		
am pm	oz./ R min. L		
am pm	oz./ R min. L		

Notes

Naps

start	finish

Baby A

Time	Breast/Bottle	Diaper	Meds
am pm	oz./ R min. L		
am pm	oz./ R min. L		
am pm	oz./ R min. L		
am pm	oz./ R min. L		
am pm	oz./ R min. L		
am pm	oz./ R min. L		
am pm	oz./ R min. L		
am pm	oz./ R min. L		

Notes

Naps

start	finish

TODAY IS:

twin tracker

twin tracker

To Do

Reminders

Baby A

Time	Breast/Bottle	Diaper	Meds
am pm	oz./R min. L		
am pm	oz./R min. L		
am pm	oz./R min. L		
am pm	oz./R min. L		
am pm	oz./R min. L		
am pm	oz./R min. L		
am pm	oz./R min. L		
am pm	oz./R min. L		

Naps

start	finish

Notes

Baby B

Time	Breast/Bottle	Diaper	Meds
am pm	oz./R min. L		
am pm	oz./R min. L		
am pm	oz./R min. L		
am pm	oz./R min. L		
am pm	oz./R min. L		
am pm	oz./R min. L		
am pm	oz./R min. L		
am pm	oz./R min. L		

Naps

start	finish

Notes

TODAY IS:

twin tracker

To Do

Reminders

Baby A

Time	Breast/Bottle	Diaper	Meds
am pm	oz./R min. L		
am pm	oz./R min. L		
am pm	oz./R min. L		
am pm	oz./R min. L		
am pm	oz./R min. L		
am pm	oz./R min. L		
am pm	oz./R min. L		

Naps
start	finish

Notes

Baby B

Time	Breast/Bottle	Diaper	Meds
am pm	oz./R min. L		
am pm	oz./R min. L		
am pm	oz./R min. L		
am pm	oz./R min. L		
am pm	oz./R min. L		
am pm	oz./R min. L		
am pm	oz./R min. L		

Naps
start	finish

Notes

TODAY IS:

twin tracker

To Do

Reminders

Baby A

Time		Breast/Bottle		Diaper	Meds
am pm		oz./R min. L			
am pm		oz./R min. L			
am pm		oz./R min. L			
am pm		oz./R min. L			
am pm		oz./R min. L			
am pm		oz./R min. L			
am pm		oz./R min. L			
am pm		oz./R min. L			

Naps

start	finish

Notes

Baby B

Time		Breast/Bottle		Diaper	Meds
am pm		oz./R min. L			
am pm		oz./R min. L			
am pm		oz./R min. L			
am pm		oz./R min. L			
am pm		oz./R min. L			
am pm		oz./R min. L			
am pm		oz./R min. L			
am pm		oz./R min. L			

Naps

start	finish

Notes

TODAY IS:

To Do

Reminders

Baby B

Time	Breast/Bottle	Diaper	Meds
am pm	oz. / R min. L		
am pm	oz. / R min. L		
am pm	oz. / R min. L		
am pm	oz. / R min. L		
am pm	oz. / R min. L		
am pm	oz. / R min. L		
am pm	oz. / R min. L		
am pm	oz. / R min. L		

Naps

start	finish

Notes

Baby A

Time	Breast/Bottle	Diaper	Meds
am pm	oz. / R min. L		
am pm	oz. / R min. L		
am pm	oz. / R min. L		
am pm	oz. / R min. L		
am pm	oz. / R min. L		
am pm	oz. / R min. L		
am pm	oz. / R min. L		
am pm	oz. / R min. L		

Naps

start	finish

Notes

twin tracker

TODAY IS:

To Do

Reminders

Baby B

Time	Breast/Bottle	Diaper	Meds
am pm	oz./R min. L		
am pm	oz./R min. L		
am pm	oz./R min. L		
am pm	oz./R min. L		
am pm	oz./R min. L		
am pm	oz./R min. L		
am pm	oz./R min. L		
am pm	oz./R min. L		

Notes

Naps

start	finish

Baby A

Time	Breast/Bottle	Diaper	Meds
am pm	oz./R min. L		
am pm	oz./R min. L		
am pm	oz./R min. L		
am pm	oz./R min. L		
am pm	oz./R min. L		
am pm	oz./R min. L		
am pm	oz./R min. L		
am pm	oz./R min. L		

Notes

Naps

start	finish

TODAY IS:

twin tracker

twin tracker

To Do

Reminders

Baby B

Time	Breast/Bottle		Diaper	Meds
am / pm	oz. / R	min. L		
am / pm	oz. / R	min. L		
am / pm	oz. / R	min. L		
am / pm	oz. / R	min. L		
am / pm	oz. / R	min. L		
am / pm	oz. / R	min. L		
am / pm	oz. / R	min. L		
am / pm	oz. / R	min. L		

Naps

start	finish

Notes

Baby A

Time	Breast/Bottle		Diaper	Meds
am / pm	oz. / R	min. L		
am / pm	oz. / R	min. L		
am / pm	oz. / R	min. L		
am / pm	oz. / R	min. L		
am / pm	oz. / R	min. L		
am / pm	oz. / R	min. L		
am / pm	oz. / R	min. L		
am / pm	oz. / R	min. L		

Naps

start	finish

Notes

TODAY IS:

To Do

Reminders

Baby B

Time		Breast/Bottle	Diaper	Meds
am pm		oz./R min. L		
am pm		oz./R min. L		
am pm		oz./R min. L		
am pm		oz./R min. L		
am pm		oz./R min. L		
am pm		oz./R min. L		
am pm		oz./R min. L		
am pm		oz./R min. L		

Naps
start	finish

Notes

Baby A

Time		Breast/Bottle	Diaper	Meds
am pm		oz./R min. L		
am pm		oz./R min. L		
am pm		oz./R min. L		
am pm		oz./R min. L		
am pm		oz./R min. L		
am pm		oz./R min. L		
am pm		oz./R min. L		
am pm		oz./R min. L		

Naps
start	finish

Notes

TODAY IS:

twin tracker

twin tracker

To Do

Baby A

Time		Breast/Bottle		Diaper	Meds
am pm		oz. / R min. L			
am pm		oz. / R min. L			
am pm		oz. / R min. L			
am pm		oz. / R min. L			
am pm		oz. / R min. L			
am pm		oz. / R min. L			
am pm		oz. / R min. L			
am pm		oz. / R min. L			

Naps

start	finish

Notes

Baby B

Time		Breast/Bottle		Diaper	Meds
am pm		oz. / R min. L			
am pm		oz. / R min. L			
am pm		oz. / R min. L			
am pm		oz. / R min. L			
am pm		oz. / R min. L			
am pm		oz. / R min. L			
am pm		oz. / R min. L			
am pm		oz. / R min. L			

Naps

start	finish

Notes

Reminders

TODAY IS:

twin tracker

To Do

Reminders

Baby A

Time	Breast/Bottle	Diaper	Meds
am pm	oz. / R min. L		
am pm	oz. / R min. L		
am pm	oz. / R min. L		
am pm	oz. / R min. L		
am pm	oz. / R min. L		
am pm	oz. / R min. L		
am pm	oz. / R min. L		
am pm	oz. / R min. L		

Naps
start	finish

Notes

Baby B

Time	Breast/Bottle	Diaper	Meds
am pm	oz. / R min. L		
am pm	oz. / R min. L		
am pm	oz. / R min. L		
am pm	oz. / R min. L		
am pm	oz. / R min. L		
am pm	oz. / R min. L		
am pm	oz. / R min. L		
am pm	oz. / R min. L		

Naps
start	finish

Notes

TODAY IS:

twin tracker

To Do

Reminders

Baby B

Time	Breast/Bottle	Diaper	Meds
am / pm	oz. / R min. L		
am / pm	oz. / R min. L		
am / pm	oz. / R min. L		
am / pm	oz. / R min. L		
am / pm	oz. / R min. L		
am / pm	oz. / R min. L		
am / pm	oz. / R min. L		
am / pm	oz. / R min. L		

Naps

start	finish

Notes

Baby A

Time	Breast/Bottle	Diaper	Meds
am / pm	oz. / R min. L		
am / pm	oz. / R min. L		
am / pm	oz. / R min. L		
am / pm	oz. / R min. L		
am / pm	oz. / R min. L		
am / pm	oz. / R min. L		
am / pm	oz. / R min. L		
am / pm	oz. / R min. L		

Naps

start	finish

Notes

TODAY IS:

To Do

Reminders

Baby B

Time	Breast/Bottle	Diaper	Meds
am pm	oz./R min. L		
am pm	oz./R min. L		
am pm	oz./R min. L		
am pm	oz./R min. L		
am pm	oz./R min. L		
am pm	oz./R min. L		
am pm	oz./R min. L		
am pm	oz./R min. L		

Notes

Naps

start	finish

Baby A

Time	Breast/Bottle	Diaper	Meds
am pm	oz./R min. L		
am pm	oz./R min. L		
am pm	oz./R min. L		
am pm	oz./R min. L		
am pm	oz./R min. L		
am pm	oz./R min. L		
am pm	oz./R min. L		
am pm	oz./R min. L		

Notes

Naps

start	finish

TODAY IS:

twin tracker

twin tracker

To Do

Reminders

Baby B

Time	Breast/Bottle	Diaper	Meds
am pm	oz./ R min. L		
am pm	oz./ R min. L		
am pm	oz./ R min. L		
am pm	oz./ R min. L		
am pm	oz./ R min. L		
am pm	oz./ R min. L		
am pm	oz./ R min. L		
am pm	oz./ R min. L		

Naps

start	finish

Notes

Baby A

Time	Breast/Bottle	Diaper	Meds
am pm	oz./ R min. L		
am pm	oz./ R min. L		
am pm	oz./ R min. L		
am pm	oz./ R min. L		
am pm	oz./ R min. L		
am pm	oz./ R min. L		
am pm	oz./ R min. L		

Naps

start	finish

Notes

TODAY IS:

To Do

Reminders

Baby B

Time	Breast/Bottle	Diaper	Meds
am pm	oz. / R min. L		
am pm	oz. / R min. L		
am pm	oz. / R min. L		
am pm	oz. / R min. L		
am pm	oz. / R min. L		
am pm	oz. / R min. L		
am pm	oz. / R min. L		
am pm	oz. / R min. L		

Naps

start	finish

Notes

Baby A

Time	Breast/Bottle	Diaper	Meds
am pm	oz. / R min. L		
am pm	oz. / R min. L		
am pm	oz. / R min. L		
am pm	oz. / R min. L		
am pm	oz. / R min. L		
am pm	oz. / R min. L		
am pm	oz. / R min. L		

Naps

start	finish

Notes

twin tracker

TODAY IS:

twin tracker

To Do

Reminders

Baby A

Time	Breast/Bottle	Diaper	Meds
am pm	oz./R min. L		
am pm	oz./R min. L		
am pm	oz./R min. L		
am pm	oz./R min. L		
am pm	oz./R min. L		
am pm	oz./R min. L		
am pm	oz./R min. L		
am pm	oz./R min. L		

Naps
start	finish

Notes

Baby B

Time	Breast/Bottle	Diaper	Meds
am pm	oz./R min. L		
am pm	oz./R min. L		
am pm	oz./R min. L		
am pm	oz./R min. L		
am pm	oz./R min. L		
am pm	oz./R min. L		
am pm	oz./R min. L		
am pm	oz./R min. L		

Naps
start	finish

Notes

TODAY IS:

To Do

Reminders

Baby B

Time		Breast/Bottle		Diaper	Meds
am pm		oz. / R min. L			
am pm		oz. / R min. L			
am pm		oz. / R min. L			
am pm		oz. / R min. L			
am pm		oz. / R min. L			
am pm		oz. / R min. L			
am pm		oz. / R min. L			
am pm		oz. / R min. L			

Notes

Naps

start	finish

Baby A

Time		Breast/Bottle		Diaper	Meds
am pm		oz. / R min. L			
am pm		oz. / R min. L			
am pm		oz. / R min. L			
am pm		oz. / R min. L			
am pm		oz. / R min. L			
am pm		oz. / R min. L			
am pm		oz. / R min. L			
am pm		oz. / R min. L			

Notes

Naps

start	finish

TODAY IS:

twin tracker

twin tracker

To Do

Baby A

Time	Breast/Bottle		Diaper	Meds
am pm	oz. / R	min. L		
am pm	oz. / R	min. L		
am pm	oz. / R	min. L		
am pm	oz. / R	min. L		
am pm	oz. / R	min. L		
am pm	oz. / R	min. L		
am pm	oz. / R	min. L		
am pm	oz. / R	min. L		

Naps

start	finish

Notes

Baby B

Time	Breast/Bottle		Diaper	Meds
am pm	oz. / R	min. L		
am pm	oz. / R	min. L		
am pm	oz. / R	min. L		
am pm	oz. / R	min. L		
am pm	oz. / R	min. L		
am pm	oz. / R	min. L		
am pm	oz. / R	min. L		
am pm	oz. / R	min. L		

Naps

start	finish

Notes

Reminders

TODAY IS:

To Do

Reminders

Baby B

Time	Breast/Bottle	Diaper	Meds
am pm	oz. / R min. L		
am pm	oz. / R min. L		
am pm	oz. / R min. L		
am pm	oz. / R min. L		
am pm	oz. / R min. L		
am pm	oz. / R min. L		
am pm	oz. / R min. L		
am pm	oz. / R min. L		

Naps

start	finish

Notes

Baby A

Time	Breast/Bottle	Diaper	Meds
am pm	oz. / R min. L		
am pm	oz. / R min. L		
am pm	oz. / R min. L		
am pm	oz. / R min. L		
am pm	oz. / R min. L		
am pm	oz. / R min. L		
am pm	oz. / R min. L		
am pm	oz. / R min. L		

Naps

start	finish

Notes

TODAY IS:

twin tracker

twin tracker

To Do

Reminders

Baby A

Time	Breast/Bottle		Diaper	Meds
am pm	oz. / R	min. L		
am pm	oz. / R	min. L		
am pm	oz. / R	min. L		
am pm	oz. / R	min. L		
am pm	oz. / R	min. L		
am pm	oz. / R	min. L		
am pm	oz. / R	min. L		

Naps
start	finish

Notes

Baby B

Time	Breast/Bottle		Diaper	Meds
am pm	oz. / R	min. L		
am pm	oz. / R	min. L		
am pm	oz. / R	min. L		
am pm	oz. / R	min. L		
am pm	oz. / R	min. L		
am pm	oz. / R	min. L		
am pm	oz. / R	min. L		

Naps
start	finish

Notes

TODAY IS:

To Do

Reminders

Baby B

Time	Breast/Bottle	Diaper	Meds
am pm	oz. / R min. L		
am pm	oz. / R min. L		
am pm	oz. / R min. L		
am pm	oz. / R min. L		
am pm	oz. / R min. L		
am pm	oz. / R min. L		
am pm	oz. / R min. L		
am pm	oz. / R min. L		

Naps

start	finish

Notes

Baby A

Time	Breast/Bottle	Diaper	Meds
am pm	oz. / R min. L		
am pm	oz. / R min. L		
am pm	oz. / R min. L		
am pm	oz. / R min. L		
am pm	oz. / R min. L		
am pm	oz. / R min. L		
am pm	oz. / R min. L		
am pm	oz. / R min. L		

Naps

start	finish

Notes

TODAY IS:

twin tracker

twin tracker

To Do

Reminders

TODAY IS:

Baby A

Time	Breast/Bottle	Diaper	Meds
am pm	oz. / R min. L		
am pm	oz. / R min. L		
am pm	oz. / R min. L		
am pm	oz. / R min. L		
am pm	oz. / R min. L		
am pm	oz. / R min. L		
am pm	oz. / R min. L		
am pm	oz. / R min. L		

Naps

start	finish

Notes

Baby B

Time	Breast/Bottle	Diaper	Meds
am pm	oz. / R min. L		
am pm	oz. / R min. L		
am pm	oz. / R min. L		
am pm	oz. / R min. L		
am pm	oz. / R min. L		
am pm	oz. / R min. L		
am pm	oz. / R min. L		
am pm	oz. / R min. L		

Naps

start	finish

Notes

twin tracker

To Do

Reminders

Baby B

Time	Breast/Bottle	Diaper	Meds
am pm	oz. / R min. L		
am pm	oz. / R min. L		
am pm	oz. / R min. L		
am pm	oz. / R min. L		
am pm	oz. / R min. L		
am pm	oz. / R min. L		
am pm	oz. / R min. L		
am pm	oz. / R min. L		

Naps

start	finish

Notes

Baby A

Time	Breast/Bottle	Diaper	Meds
am pm	oz. / R min. L		
am pm	oz. / R min. L		
am pm	oz. / R min. L		
am pm	oz. / R min. L		
am pm	oz. / R min. L		
am pm	oz. / R min. L		
am pm	oz. / R min. L		
am pm	oz. / R min. L		

Naps

start	finish

Notes

TODAY IS:

twin tracker

To Do

Reminders

Baby A

Time	Breast/Bottle	Diaper	Meds
am / pm	oz. / R _ min. L		
am / pm	oz. / R _ min. L		
am / pm	oz. / R _ min. L		
am / pm	oz. / R _ min. L		
am / pm	oz. / R _ min. L		
am / pm	oz. / R _ min. L		
am / pm	oz. / R _ min. L		
am / pm	oz. / R _ min. L		

Naps

start	finish

Notes

Baby B

Time	Breast/Bottle	Diaper	Meds
am / pm	oz. / R _ min. L		
am / pm	oz. / R _ min. L		
am / pm	oz. / R _ min. L		
am / pm	oz. / R _ min. L		
am / pm	oz. / R _ min. L		
am / pm	oz. / R _ min. L		
am / pm	oz. / R _ min. L		
am / pm	oz. / R _ min. L		

Naps

start	finish

Notes

TODAY IS:

To Do

Reminders

Baby B

Time	Breast/Bottle		Diaper	Meds
am pm	oz./R	min. L		
am pm	oz./R	min. L		
am pm	oz./R	min. L		
am pm	oz./R	min. L		
am pm	oz./R	min. L		
am pm	oz./R	min. L		
am pm	oz./R	min. L		
am pm	oz./R	min. L		

Naps

start	finish

Notes

Baby A

Time	Breast/Bottle		Diaper	Meds
am pm	oz./R	min. L		
am pm	oz./R	min. L		
am pm	oz./R	min. L		
am pm	oz./R	min. L		
am pm	oz./R	min. L		
am pm	oz./R	min. L		
am pm	oz./R	min. L		
am pm	oz./R	min. L		

Naps

start	finish

Notes

twin tracker

TODAY IS:

twin tracker

To Do

Reminders

Baby A

Time	Breast/Bottle	Diaper	Meds
am pm	oz. / R min. L		
am pm	oz. / R min. L		
am pm	oz. / R min. L		
am pm	oz. / R min. L		
am pm	oz. / R min. L		
am pm	oz. / R min. L		
am pm	oz. / R min. L		
am pm	oz. / R min. L		

Naps

start	finish

Notes

Baby B

Time	Breast/Bottle	Diaper	Meds
am pm	oz. / R min. L		
am pm	oz. / R min. L		
am pm	oz. / R min. L		
am pm	oz. / R min. L		
am pm	oz. / R min. L		
am pm	oz. / R min. L		
am pm	oz. / R min. L		
am pm	oz. / R min. L		

Naps

start	finish

Notes

TODAY IS:

twin tracker

To Do

Reminders

Baby A

Time	Breast/Bottle	Diaper	Meds
am pm	oz./R min. L		
am pm	oz./R min. L		
am pm	oz./R min. L		
am pm	oz./R min. L		
am pm	oz./R min. L		
am pm	oz./R min. L		
am pm	oz./R min. L		
am pm	oz./R min. L		

Naps

start	finish

Notes

Baby B

Time	Breast/Bottle	Diaper	Meds
am pm	oz./R min. L		
am pm	oz./R min. L		
am pm	oz./R min. L		
am pm	oz./R min. L		
am pm	oz./R min. L		
am pm	oz./R min. L		
am pm	oz./R min. L		
am pm	oz./R min. L		

Naps

start	finish

Notes

TODAY IS:

To Do

Reminders

Baby B

Time	Breast/Bottle	Diaper	Meds
am pm	oz./R min. L		
am pm	oz./R min. L		
am pm	oz./R min. L		
am pm	oz./R min. L		
am pm	oz./R min. L		
am pm	oz./R min. L		
am pm	oz./R min. L		
am pm	oz./R min. L		

Naps

start	finish

Notes

Baby A

Time	Breast/Bottle	Diaper	Meds
am pm	oz./R min. L		
am pm	oz./R min. L		
am pm	oz./R min. L		
am pm	oz./R min. L		
am pm	oz./R min. L		
am pm	oz./R min. L		
am pm	oz./R min. L		
am pm	oz./R min. L		

Naps

start	finish

Notes

TODAY IS:

twin tracker

twin tracker

To Do

Reminders

Baby B

Time		Breast/Bottle	Diaper	Meds
am pm		oz. / R min. L		
am pm		oz. / R min. L		
am pm		oz. / R min. L		
am pm		oz. / R min. L		
am pm		oz. / R min. L		
am pm		oz. / R min. L		
am pm		oz. / R min. L		
am pm		oz. / R min. L		

Naps
start	finish

Notes

Baby A

Time		Breast/Bottle	Diaper	Meds
am pm		oz. / R min. L		
am pm		oz. / R min. L		
am pm		oz. / R min. L		
am pm		oz. / R min. L		
am pm		oz. / R min. L		
am pm		oz. / R min. L		
am pm		oz. / R min. L		
am pm		oz. / R min. L		

Naps
start	finish

Notes

TODAY IS:

twin tracker

To Do

Reminders

Baby A

Time	Breast/Bottle		Diaper	Meds
am pm	oz./R min. L			
am pm	oz./R min. L			
am pm	oz./R min. L			
am pm	oz./R min. L			
am pm	oz./R min. L			
am pm	oz./R min. L			
am pm	oz./R min. L			
am pm	oz./R min. L			

Naps
start	finish

Notes

Baby B

Time	Breast/Bottle		Diaper	Meds
am pm	oz./R min. L			
am pm	oz./R min. L			
am pm	oz./R min. L			
am pm	oz./R min. L			
am pm	oz./R min. L			
am pm	oz./R min. L			
am pm	oz./R min. L			
am pm	oz./R min. L			

Naps
start	finish

Notes

TODAY IS:

twin tracker

To Do

Reminders

Baby A

Time	Breast/Bottle	Diaper	Meds
am pm	oz./R min. L		
am pm	oz./R min. L		
am pm	oz./R min. L		
am pm	oz./R min. L		
am pm	oz./R min. L		
am pm	oz./R min. L		
am pm	oz./R min. L		
am pm	oz./R min. L		

Naps

start	finish

Notes

Baby B

Time	Breast/Bottle	Diaper	Meds
am pm	oz./R min. L		
am pm	oz./R min. L		
am pm	oz./R min. L		
am pm	oz./R min. L		
am pm	oz./R min. L		
am pm	oz./R min. L		
am pm	oz./R min. L		
am pm	oz./R min. L		

Naps

start	finish

Notes

TODAY IS:

twin tracker

Baby A

Time	Breast/Bottle		Diaper	Meds
am pm	oz./R min. L			
am pm	oz./R min. L			
am pm	oz./R min. L			
am pm	oz./R min. L			
am pm	oz./R min. L			
am pm	oz./R min. L			
am pm	oz./R min. L			
am pm	oz./R min. L			

Naps

start		finish		

Notes

Baby B

Time	Breast/Bottle		Diaper	Meds
am pm	oz./R min. L			
am pm	oz./R min. L			
am pm	oz./R min. L			
am pm	oz./R min. L			
am pm	oz./R min. L			
am pm	oz./R min. L			
am pm	oz./R min. L			
am pm	oz./R min. L			

Naps

start		finish		

Notes

To Do

Reminders

TODAY IS:

To Do

Reminders

Baby B

Time	Breast/Bottle		Diaper	Meds
am pm	oz. / R	min. L		
am pm	oz. / R	min. L		
am pm	oz. / R	min. L		
am pm	oz. / R	min. L		
am pm	oz. / R	min. L		
am pm	oz. / R	min. L		
am pm	oz. / R	min. L		
am pm	oz. / R	min. L		

Naps
start	finish

Notes

Baby A

Time	Breast/Bottle		Diaper	Meds
am pm	oz. / R	min. L		
am pm	oz. / R	min. L		
am pm	oz. / R	min. L		
am pm	oz. / R	min. L		
am pm	oz. / R	min. L		
am pm	oz. / R	min. L		
am pm	oz. / R	min. L		
am pm	oz. / R	min. L		

Naps
start	finish

Notes

TODAY IS:

twin tracker

To Do

Baby B

Time		Breast/Bottle		Diaper	Meds
am / pm		oz./R min. L			
am / pm		oz./R min. L			
am / pm		oz./R min. L			
am / pm		oz./R min. L			
am / pm		oz./R min. L			
am / pm		oz./R min. L			
am / pm		oz./R min. L			
am / pm		oz./R min. L			

Naps

start	finish

Notes

Baby A

Time		Breast/Bottle		Diaper	Meds
am / pm		oz./R min. L			
am / pm		oz./R min. L			
am / pm		oz./R min. L			
am / pm		oz./R min. L			
am / pm		oz./R min. L			
am / pm		oz./R min. L			
am / pm		oz./R min. L			
am / pm		oz./R min. L			

Naps

start	finish

Notes

Reminders

TODAY IS:

twin tracker

twin tracker

To Do

Reminders

Baby B

Time	Breast/Bottle	Diaper	Meds
am pm	oz./R min. L		
am pm	oz./R min. L		
am pm	oz./R min. L		
am pm	oz./R min. L		
am pm	oz./R min. L		
am pm	oz./R min. L		
am pm	oz./R min. L		
am pm	oz./R min. L		

Naps

start	finish

Notes

Baby A

Time	Breast/Bottle	Diaper	Meds
am pm	oz./R min. L		
am pm	oz./R min. L		
am pm	oz./R min. L		
am pm	oz./R min. L		
am pm	oz./R min. L		
am pm	oz./R min. L		
am pm	oz./R min. L		
am pm	oz./R min. L		

Naps

start	finish

Notes

TODAY IS:

twin tracker

To Do

Reminders

Baby B

Time	Breast/Bottle		Diaper	Meds
	oz./R	min. L		
am pm				
am pm				
am pm				
am pm				
am pm				
am pm				
am pm				
am pm				

Baby A

Time	Breast/Bottle		Diaper	Meds
	oz./R	min. L		
am pm				
am pm				
am pm				
am pm				
am pm				
am pm				
am pm				
am pm				

Notes

Naps

start	finish

Notes

Naps

start	finish

TODAY IS:

To Do

Reminders

Baby B

Time	Breast/Bottle	Diaper	Meds
am / pm	oz. / R min. L		
am / pm	oz. / R min. L		
am / pm	oz. / R min. L		
am / pm	oz. / R min. L		
am / pm	oz. / R min. L		
am / pm	oz. / R min. L		
am / pm	oz. / R min. L		
am / pm	oz. / R min. L		

Naps

start	finish

Notes

Baby A

Time	Breast/Bottle	Diaper	Meds
am / pm	oz. / R min. L		
am / pm	oz. / R min. L		
am / pm	oz. / R min. L		
am / pm	oz. / R min. L		
am / pm	oz. / R min. L		
am / pm	oz. / R min. L		
am / pm	oz. / R min. L		
am / pm	oz. / R min. L		

Naps

start	finish

Notes

TODAY IS:

twin tracker

twin tracker

To Do

Reminders

Baby A

Time		Breast/Bottle	Diaper	Meds
am pm	oz. / R min. L			
am pm	oz. / R min. L			
am pm	oz. / R min. L			
am pm	oz. / R min. L			
am pm	oz. / R min. L			
am pm	oz. / R min. L			
am pm	oz. / R min. L			
am pm	oz. / R min. L			

Naps

start	finish

Notes

Baby B

Time		Breast/Bottle	Diaper	Meds
am pm	oz. / R min. L			
am pm	oz. / R min. L			
am pm	oz. / R min. L			
am pm	oz. / R min. L			
am pm	oz. / R min. L			
am pm	oz. / R min. L			
am pm	oz. / R min. L			
am pm	oz. / R min. L			

Naps

start	finish

Notes

TODAY IS:

To Do

Reminders

Baby B

Time	Breast/Bottle	Diaper	Meds
am pm	oz./R min. L		
am pm	oz./R min. L		
am pm	oz./R min. L		
am pm	oz./R min. L		
am pm	oz./R min. L		
am pm	oz./R min. L		
am pm	oz./R min. L		
am pm	oz./R min. L		

Naps

start	finish

Notes

Baby A

Time	Breast/Bottle	Diaper	Meds
am pm	oz./R min. L		
am pm	oz./R min. L		
am pm	oz./R min. L		
am pm	oz./R min. L		
am pm	oz./R min. L		
am pm	oz./R min. L		
am pm	oz./R min. L		
am pm	oz./R min. L		

Naps

start	finish

Notes

TODAY IS:

twin tracker

twin tracker

To Do

Reminders

Baby A

Time	Breast/Bottle		Diaper	Meds
	oz./R	min. L		
am pm				
am pm				
am pm				
am pm				
am pm				
am pm				
am pm				
am pm				

Notes

Naps

start	finish

Baby B

Time	Breast/Bottle		Diaper	Meds
	oz./R	min. L		
am pm				
am pm				
am pm				
am pm				
am pm				
am pm				
am pm				
am pm				

Notes

Naps

start	finish

TODAY IS:

twin tracker

To Do

Reminders

Baby A

Time		Breast/Bottle	Diaper	Meds
am / pm	oz. / R min. L			
am / pm	oz. / R min. L			
am / pm	oz. / R min. L			
am / pm	oz. / R min. L			
am / pm	oz. / R min. L			
am / pm	oz. / R min. L			
am / pm	oz. / R min. L			
am / pm	oz. / R min. L			

Naps

start	finish

Notes

Baby B

Time		Breast/Bottle	Diaper	Meds
am / pm	oz. / R min. L			
am / pm	oz. / R min. L			
am / pm	oz. / R min. L			
am / pm	oz. / R min. L			
am / pm	oz. / R min. L			
am / pm	oz. / R min. L			
am / pm	oz. / R min. L			
am / pm	oz. / R min. L			

Naps

start	finish

Notes

TODAY IS:

twin tracker

To Do

Reminders

Baby A

Time	Breast/Bottle	Diaper	Meds
am pm	oz. / R min. L		
am pm	oz. / R min. L		
am pm	oz. / R min. L		
am pm	oz. / R min. L		
am pm	oz. / R min. L		
am pm	oz. / R min. L		
am pm	oz. / R min. L		
am pm	oz. / R min. L		

Naps

start	finish

Notes

Baby B

Time	Breast/Bottle	Diaper	Meds
am pm	oz. / R min. L		
am pm	oz. / R min. L		
am pm	oz. / R min. L		
am pm	oz. / R min. L		
am pm	oz. / R min. L		
am pm	oz. / R min. L		
am pm	oz. / R min. L		
am pm	oz. / R min. L		

Naps

start	finish

Notes

TODAY IS:

To Do

Reminders

Baby B

Time	Breast/ Bottle		Diaper	Meds
am pm	oz./ R min. L			
am pm	oz./ R min. L			
am pm	oz./ R min. L			
am pm	oz./ R min. L			
am pm	oz./ R min. L			
am pm	oz./ R min. L			
am pm	oz./ R min. L			
am pm	oz./ R min. L			

Naps
start	finish

Notes

Baby A

Time	Breast/ Bottle		Diaper	Meds
am pm	oz./ R min. L			
am pm	oz./ R min. L			
am pm	oz./ R min. L			
am pm	oz./ R min. L			
am pm	oz./ R min. L			
am pm	oz./ R min. L			
am pm	oz./ R min. L			

Naps
start	finish

Notes

TODAY IS:

twin tracker

To Do

Baby A

Time	Breast/Bottle	Diaper	Meds
am / pm	oz. / R min. L		
am / pm	oz. / R min. L		
am / pm	oz. / R min. L		
am / pm	oz. / R min. L		
am / pm	oz. / R min. L		
am / pm	oz. / R min. L		
am / pm	oz. / R min. L		
am / pm	oz. / R min. L		

Naps

start	finish

Notes

Baby B

Time	Breast/Bottle	Diaper	Meds
am / pm	oz. / R min. L		
am / pm	oz. / R min. L		
am / pm	oz. / R min. L		
am / pm	oz. / R min. L		
am / pm	oz. / R min. L		
am / pm	oz. / R min. L		
am / pm	oz. / R min. L		
am / pm	oz. / R min. L		

Naps

start	finish

Notes

Reminders

TODAY IS:

twin tracker

twin tracker

To Do

Reminders

Baby B

Time		Breast/Bottle		Diaper	Meds
am pm		oz./R min. L			
am pm		oz./R min. L			
am pm		oz./R min. L			
am pm		oz./R min. L			
am pm		oz./R min. L			
am pm		oz./R min. L			
am pm		oz./R min. L			
am pm		oz./R min. L			

Naps
start		finish	

Notes

Baby A

Time		Breast/Bottle		Diaper	Meds
am pm		oz./R min. L			
am pm		oz./R min. L			
am pm		oz./R min. L			
am pm		oz./R min. L			
am pm		oz./R min. L			
am pm		oz./R min. L			
am pm		oz./R min. L			
am pm		oz./R min. L			

Naps
start		finish	

Notes

TODAY IS:

To Do

Reminders

Baby B

Time	Breast/Bottle	Diaper	Meds
am pm	oz./R min. L		
am pm	oz./R min. L		
am pm	oz./R min. L		
am pm	oz./R min. L		
am pm	oz./R min. L		
am pm	oz./R min. L		
am pm	oz./R min. L		
am pm	oz./R min. L		

Notes

Naps

start	finish

Baby A

Time	Breast/Bottle	Diaper	Meds
am pm	oz./R min. L		
am pm	oz./R min. L		
am pm	oz./R min. L		
am pm	oz./R min. L		
am pm	oz./R min. L		
am pm	oz./R min. L		
am pm	oz./R min. L		
am pm	oz./R min. L		

Notes

Naps

start	finish

TODAY IS:

twin tracker

To Do

Reminders

Baby A

Time		Breast/Bottle		Diaper	Meds
am / pm		oz. / R, min. L			
am / pm		oz. / R, min. L			
am / pm		oz. / R, min. L			
am / pm		oz. / R, min. L			
am / pm		oz. / R, min. L			
am / pm		oz. / R, min. L			
am / pm		oz. / R, min. L			
am / pm		oz. / R, min. L			

Naps

start	finish

Notes

Baby B

Time		Breast/Bottle		Diaper	Meds
am / pm		oz. / R, min. L			
am / pm		oz. / R, min. L			
am / pm		oz. / R, min. L			
am / pm		oz. / R, min. L			
am / pm		oz. / R, min. L			
am / pm		oz. / R, min. L			
am / pm		oz. / R, min. L			
am / pm		oz. / R, min. L			

Naps

start	finish

Notes

TODAY IS:

twin tracker

To Do

Baby A

Time	Breast/Bottle	Diaper	Meds
am / pm	oz. / R / min. L		
am / pm	oz. / R / min. L		
am / pm	oz. / R / min. L		
am / pm	oz. / R / min. L		
am / pm	oz. / R / min. L		
am / pm	oz. / R / min. L		
am / pm	oz. / R / min. L		
am / pm	oz. / R / min. L		

Baby B

Time	Breast/Bottle	Diaper	Meds
am / pm	oz. / R / min. L		
am / pm	oz. / R / min. L		
am / pm	oz. / R / min. L		
am / pm	oz. / R / min. L		
am / pm	oz. / R / min. L		
am / pm	oz. / R / min. L		
am / pm	oz. / R / min. L		
am / pm	oz. / R / min. L		

Naps

start	finish

Notes

Reminders

Naps

start	finish

Notes

TODAY IS:

twin tracker

twin tracker

To Do

Reminders

Baby A

Time	Breast/Bottle		Diaper	Meds
am pm	oz./R min. L			
am pm	oz./R min. L			
am pm	oz./R min. L			
am pm	oz./R min. L			
am pm	oz./R min. L			
am pm	oz./R min. L			
am pm	oz./R min. L			
am pm	oz./R min. L			

Naps

start	finish

Notes

Baby B

Time	Breast/Bottle		Diaper	Meds
am pm	oz./R min. L			
am pm	oz./R min. L			
am pm	oz./R min. L			
am pm	oz./R min. L			
am pm	oz./R min. L			
am pm	oz./R min. L			
am pm	oz./R min. L			
am pm	oz./R min. L			

Naps

start	finish

Notes

TODAY IS:

twin tracker

To Do

Reminders

Baby A

Time	Breast/Bottle	Diaper	Meds
am pm	oz./R min. L		
am pm	oz./R min. L		
am pm	oz./R min. L		
am pm	oz./R min. L		
am pm	oz./R min. L		
am pm	oz./R min. L		
am pm	oz./R min. L		
am pm	oz./R min. L		

Naps
start	finish

Notes

Baby B

Time	Breast/Bottle	Diaper	Meds
am pm	oz./R min. L		
am pm	oz./R min. L		
am pm	oz./R min. L		
am pm	oz./R min. L		
am pm	oz./R min. L		
am pm	oz./R min. L		
am pm	oz./R min. L		
am pm	oz./R min. L		

Naps
start	finish

Notes

TODAY IS:

twin tracker

To Do

Reminders

Baby A

Time	Breast/Bottle	Diaper	Meds
am pm	oz. / R min. L		
am pm	oz. / R min. L		
am pm	oz. / R min. L		
am pm	oz. / R min. L		
am pm	oz. / R min. L		
am pm	oz. / R min. L		
am pm	oz. / R min. L		
am pm	oz. / R min. L		

Naps

start	finish

Notes

Baby B

Time	Breast/Bottle	Diaper	Meds
am pm	oz. / R min. L		
am pm	oz. / R min. L		
am pm	oz. / R min. L		
am pm	oz. / R min. L		
am pm	oz. / R min. L		
am pm	oz. / R min. L		
am pm	oz. / R min. L		
am pm	oz. / R min. L		

Naps

start	finish

Notes

TODAY IS:

To Do

Reminders

Baby B

Time	Breast/Bottle		Diaper	Meds
am pm	oz./R min. L			
am pm	oz./R min. L			
am pm	oz./R min. L			
am pm	oz./R min. L			
am pm	oz./R min. L			
am pm	oz./R min. L			
am pm	oz./R min. L			
am pm	oz./R min. L			

Naps
start	finish

Notes

Baby A

Time	Breast/Bottle		Diaper	Meds
am pm	oz./R min. L			
am pm	oz./R min. L			
am pm	oz./R min. L			
am pm	oz./R min. L			
am pm	oz./R min. L			
am pm	oz./R min. L			
am pm	oz./R min. L			
am pm	oz./R min. L			

Naps
start	finish

Notes

TODAY IS:

twin tracker

twin tracker

To Do

Reminders

Baby A

Time	Breast/Bottle	Diaper	Meds
am / pm	oz. / R min. / L		
am / pm	oz. / R min. / L		
am / pm	oz. / R min. / L		
am / pm	oz. / R min. / L		
am / pm	oz. / R min. / L		
am / pm	oz. / R min. / L		
am / pm	oz. / R min. / L		
am / pm	oz. / R min. / L		

Naps

start	finish

Notes

Baby B

Time	Breast/Bottle	Diaper	Meds
am / pm	oz. / R min. / L		
am / pm	oz. / R min. / L		
am / pm	oz. / R min. / L		
am / pm	oz. / R min. / L		
am / pm	oz. / R min. / L		
am / pm	oz. / R min. / L		
am / pm	oz. / R min. / L		
am / pm	oz. / R min. / L		

Naps

start	finish

Notes

TODAY IS:

twin tracker

To Do

Reminders

Baby A

Time	Breast/Bottle	Diaper	Meds
am pm	oz. / R min. L		
am pm	oz. / R min. L		
am pm	oz. / R min. L		
am pm	oz. / R min. L		
am pm	oz. / R min. L		
am pm	oz. / R min. L		
am pm	oz. / R min. L		
am pm	oz. / R min. L		

Naps

start	finish

Notes

Baby B

Time	Breast/Bottle	Diaper	Meds
am pm	oz. / R min. L		
am pm	oz. / R min. L		
am pm	oz. / R min. L		
am pm	oz. / R min. L		
am pm	oz. / R min. L		
am pm	oz. / R min. L		
am pm	oz. / R min. L		
am pm	oz. / R min. L		

Naps

start	finish

Notes

TODAY IS:

To Do

Reminders

Baby B

Time	Breast/Bottle	Diaper	Meds
am pm	oz./R min. L		
am pm	oz./R min. L		
am pm	oz./R min. L		
am pm	oz./R min. L		
am pm	oz./R min. L		
am pm	oz./R min. L		
am pm	oz./R min. L		
am pm	oz./R min. L		

Naps
start	finish

Notes

Baby A

Time	Breast/Bottle	Diaper	Meds
am pm	oz./R min. L		
am pm	oz./R min. L		
am pm	oz./R min. L		
am pm	oz./R min. L		
am pm	oz./R min. L		
am pm	oz./R min. L		
am pm	oz./R min. L		
am pm	oz./R min. L		

Naps
start	finish

Notes

TODAY IS:

twin tracker

twin tracker

To Do

Baby B

Time	Breast/Bottle	Diaper	Meds
am pm	oz./ R min. L		
am pm	oz./ R min. L		
am pm	oz./ R min. L		
am pm	oz./ R min. L		
am pm	oz./ R min. L		
am pm	oz./ R min. L		
am pm	oz./ R min. L		
am pm	oz./ R min. L		

Naps
start	finish

Notes

Baby A

Time	Breast/Bottle	Diaper	Meds
am pm	oz./ R min. L		
am pm	oz./ R min. L		
am pm	oz./ R min. L		
am pm	oz./ R min. L		
am pm	oz./ R min. L		
am pm	oz./ R min. L		
am pm	oz./ R min. L		
am pm	oz./ R min. L		

Naps
start	finish

Notes

Reminders

TODAY IS:

twin tracker

To Do

Reminders

Baby A

Time	Breast/Bottle		Diaper	Meds
am pm	oz./R	min. L		
am pm	oz./R	min. L		
am pm	oz./R	min. L		
am pm	oz./R	min. L		
am pm	oz./R	min. L		
am pm	oz./R	min. L		
am pm	oz./R	min. L		
am pm	oz./R	min. L		

Naps

start	finish

Notes

Baby B

Time	Breast/Bottle		Diaper	Meds
am pm	oz./R	min. L		
am pm	oz./R	min. L		
am pm	oz./R	min. L		
am pm	oz./R	min. L		
am pm	oz./R	min. L		
am pm	oz./R	min. L		
am pm	oz./R	min. L		
am pm	oz./R	min. L		

Naps

start	finish

Notes

TODAY IS:

twin tracker

To Do

Baby B

Time	Breast/Bottle		Diaper	Meds
am pm	oz./R	min. L		
am pm	oz./R	min. L		
am pm	oz./R	min. L		
am pm	oz./R	min. L		
am pm	oz./R	min. L		
am pm	oz./R	min. L		
am pm	oz./R	min. L		
am pm	oz./R	min. L		

Baby A

Time	Breast/Bottle		Diaper	Meds
am pm	oz./R	min. L		
am pm	oz./R	min. L		
am pm	oz./R	min. L		
am pm	oz./R	min. L		
am pm	oz./R	min. L		
am pm	oz./R	min. L		
am pm	oz./R	min. L		
am pm	oz./R	min. L		

Reminders

Notes

Naps

start	finish

Notes

Naps

start	finish

TODAY IS:

To Do

Reminders

Baby B

Time	Breast/Bottle		Diaper	Meds
am pm	oz./R	min. L		
am pm	oz./R	min. L		
am pm	oz./R	min. L		
am pm	oz./R	min. L		
am pm	oz./R	min. L		
am pm	oz./R	min. L		
am pm	oz./R	min. L		
am pm	oz./R	min. L		

Naps
start	finish

Notes

Baby A

Time	Breast/Bottle		Diaper	Meds
am pm	oz./R	min. L		
am pm	oz./R	min. L		
am pm	oz./R	min. L		
am pm	oz./R	min. L		
am pm	oz./R	min. L		
am pm	oz./R	min. L		
am pm	oz./R	min. L		
am pm	oz./R	min. L		

Naps
start	finish

Notes

TODAY IS:

twin tracker

twin tracker

To Do

Baby A

Time	Breast/Bottle	Diaper	Meds
am pm	oz./R min. L		
am pm	oz./R min. L		
am pm	oz./R min. L		
am pm	oz./R min. L		
am pm	oz./R min. L		
am pm	oz./R min. L		
am pm	oz./R min. L		
am pm	oz./R min. L		

Naps

start	finish

Notes

Baby B

Time	Breast/Bottle	Diaper	Meds
am pm	oz./R min. L		
am pm	oz./R min. L		
am pm	oz./R min. L		
am pm	oz./R min. L		
am pm	oz./R min. L		
am pm	oz./R min. L		
am pm	oz./R min. L		
am pm	oz./R min. L		

Naps

start	finish

Notes

Reminders

TODAY IS:

twin tracker

To Do

Reminders

Baby B

Time		Breast/Bottle	Diaper	Meds
am pm	oz. / R min. L			
am pm	oz. / R min. L			
am pm	oz. / R min. L			
am pm	oz. / R min. L			
am pm	oz. / R min. L			
am pm	oz. / R min. L			
am pm	oz. / R min. L			
am pm	oz. / R min. L			

Naps
start	finish

Notes

Baby A

Time		Breast/Bottle	Diaper	Meds
am pm	oz. / R min. L			
am pm	oz. / R min. L			
am pm	oz. / R min. L			
am pm	oz. / R min. L			
am pm	oz. / R min. L			
am pm	oz. / R min. L			
am pm	oz. / R min. L			

Naps
start	finish

Notes

TODAY IS:

twin tracker

To Do

Reminders

Baby A

Time		Breast/Bottle	Diaper	Meds
am pm	oz. / R min. L			
am pm	oz. / R min. L			
am pm	oz. / R min. L			
am pm	oz. / R min. L			
am pm	oz. / R min. L			
am pm	oz. / R min. L			
am pm	oz. / R min. L			
am pm	oz. / R min. L			

Naps

start	finish

Notes

Baby B

Time		Breast/Bottle	Diaper	Meds
am pm	oz. / R min. L			
am pm	oz. / R min. L			
am pm	oz. / R min. L			
am pm	oz. / R min. L			
am pm	oz. / R min. L			
am pm	oz. / R min. L			
am pm	oz. / R min. L			
am pm	oz. / R min. L			

Naps

start	finish

Notes

TODAY IS:

twin tracker

To Do

Reminders

Baby B

Time	Breast/Bottle	Diaper	Meds
am pm	oz./R min. L		
am pm	oz./R min. L		
am pm	oz./R min. L		
am pm	oz./R min. L		
am pm	oz./R min. L		
am pm	oz./R min. L		
am pm	oz./R min. L		
am pm	oz./R min. L		

Naps
start	finish

Notes

Baby A

Time	Breast/Bottle	Diaper	Meds
am pm	oz./R min. L		
am pm	oz./R min. L		
am pm	oz./R min. L		
am pm	oz./R min. L		
am pm	oz./R min. L		
am pm	oz./R min. L		
am pm	oz./R min. L		
am pm	oz./R min. L		

Naps
start	finish

Notes

TODAY IS:

twin tracker

To Do

Reminders

Baby A

Time	Breast/Bottle		Diaper	Meds
am pm	oz. / R	min. L		
am pm	oz. / R	min. L		
am pm	oz. / R	min. L		
am pm	oz. / R	min. L		
am pm	oz. / R	min. L		
am pm	oz. / R	min. L		
am pm	oz. / R	min. L		
am pm	oz. / R	min. L		

Naps
start	finish

Notes

Baby B

Time	Breast/Bottle		Diaper	Meds
am pm	oz. / R	min. L		
am pm	oz. / R	min. L		
am pm	oz. / R	min. L		
am pm	oz. / R	min. L		
am pm	oz. / R	min. L		
am pm	oz. / R	min. L		
am pm	oz. / R	min. L		
am pm	oz. / R	min. L		

Naps
start	finish

Notes

TODAY IS:

To Do

Reminders

Baby B

Time	Breast/Bottle	Diaper	Meds
am pm	oz./R min. L		
am pm	oz./R min. L		
am pm	oz./R min. L		
am pm	oz./R min. L		
am pm	oz./R min. L		
am pm	oz./R min. L		
am pm	oz./R min. L		
am pm	oz./R min. L		

Naps

start	finish

Notes

Baby A

Time	Breast/Bottle	Diaper	Meds
am pm	oz./R min. L		
am pm	oz./R min. L		
am pm	oz./R min. L		
am pm	oz./R min. L		
am pm	oz./R min. L		
am pm	oz./R min. L		
am pm	oz./R min. L		
am pm	oz./R min. L		

Naps

start	finish

Notes

TODAY IS:

twin tracker

twin tracker

To Do

Reminders

Baby A

Time	Breast/Bottle	Diaper	Meds
am pm	oz./R min. L		
am pm	oz./R min. L		
am pm	oz./R min. L		
am pm	oz./R min. L		
am pm	oz./R min. L		
am pm	oz./R min. L		
am pm	oz./R min. L		
am pm	oz./R min. L		

Naps

start	finish

Notes

Baby B

Time	Breast/Bottle	Diaper	Meds
am pm	oz./R min. L		
am pm	oz./R min. L		
am pm	oz./R min. L		
am pm	oz./R min. L		
am pm	oz./R min. L		
am pm	oz./R min. L		
am pm	oz./R min. L		
am pm	oz./R min. L		

Naps

start	finish

Notes

TODAY IS:

twin tracker

To Do

Reminders

Baby A

Time	Breast/Bottle		Diaper	Meds
am pm	oz./R	min. L		
am pm	oz./R	min. L		
am pm	oz./R	min. L		
am pm	oz./R	min. L		
am pm	oz./R	min. L		
am pm	oz./R	min. L		
am pm	oz./R	min. L		
am pm	oz./R	min. L		

Naps

start	finish

Notes

Baby B

Time	Breast/Bottle		Diaper	Meds
am pm	oz./R	min. L		
am pm	oz./R	min. L		
am pm	oz./R	min. L		
am pm	oz./R	min. L		
am pm	oz./R	min. L		
am pm	oz./R	min. L		
am pm	oz./R	min. L		
am pm	oz./R	min. L		

Naps

start	finish

Notes

TODAY IS:

twin tracker

To Do

Reminders

Baby B

Time		Breast/Bottle	Diaper	Meds
am pm		oz. / R min. L		
am pm		oz. / R min. L		
am pm		oz. / R min. L		
am pm		oz. / R min. L		
am pm		oz. / R min. L		
am pm		oz. / R min. L		
am pm		oz. / R min. L		
am pm		oz. / R min. L		

Naps
start   finish

Notes

Baby A

Time		Breast/Bottle	Diaper	Meds
am pm		oz. / R min. L		
am pm		oz. / R min. L		
am pm		oz. / R min. L		
am pm		oz. / R min. L		
am pm		oz. / R min. L		
am pm		oz. / R min. L		
am pm		oz. / R min. L		
am pm		oz. / R min. L		

Naps
start   finish

Notes

TODAY IS:

To Do

Reminders

Baby B

Time	Breast/Bottle	Diaper	Meds
am pm	oz./R min. L		
am pm	oz./R min. L		
am pm	oz./R min. L		
am pm	oz./R min. L		
am pm	oz./R min. L		
am pm	oz./R min. L		
am pm	oz./R min. L		
am pm	oz./R min. L		

Baby A

Time	Breast/Bottle	Diaper	Meds
am pm	oz./R min. L		
am pm	oz./R min. L		
am pm	oz./R min. L		
am pm	oz./R min. L		
am pm	oz./R min. L		
am pm	oz./R min. L		
am pm	oz./R min. L		
am pm	oz./R min. L		

Naps

start	finish

Notes

TODAY IS:

twin tracker

twin tracker

TODAY IS:

To Do

Reminders

Baby A

Time		Breast/Bottle	Diaper	Meds
am pm		oz./R min. L		
am pm		oz./R min. L		
am pm		oz./R min. L		
am pm		oz./R min. L		
am pm		oz./R min. L		
am pm		oz./R min. L		
am pm		oz./R min. L		
am pm		oz./R min. L		

Naps

start	finish

Notes

Baby B

Time		Breast/Bottle	Diaper	Meds
am pm		oz./R min. L		
am pm		oz./R min. L		
am pm		oz./R min. L		
am pm		oz./R min. L		
am pm		oz./R min. L		
am pm		oz./R min. L		
am pm		oz./R min. L		
am pm		oz./R min. L		

Naps

start	finish

Notes

To Do

Reminders

Baby B

Time	Breast/Bottle		Diaper	Meds
am pm	oz./R min. L			
am pm	oz./R min. L			
am pm	oz./R min. L			
am pm	oz./R min. L			
am pm	oz./R min. L			
am pm	oz./R min. L			
am pm	oz./R min. L			
am pm	oz./R min. L			

Naps

start	finish

Notes

Baby A

Time	Breast/Bottle		Diaper	Meds
am pm	oz./R min. L			
am pm	oz./R min. L			
am pm	oz./R min. L			
am pm	oz./R min. L			
am pm	oz./R min. L			
am pm	oz./R min. L			
am pm	oz./R min. L			
am pm	oz./R min. L			

Naps

start	finish

Notes

TODAY IS:

twin tracker

Baby A

Time	Breast/Bottle	Diaper	Meds
am pm	oz./ R min. L		
am pm	oz./ R min. L		
am pm	oz./ R min. L		
am pm	oz./ R min. L		
am pm	oz./ R min. L		
am pm	oz./ R min. L		
am pm	oz./ R min. L		
am pm	oz./ R min. L		

Baby B

Time	Breast/Bottle	Diaper	Meds
am pm	oz./ R min. L		
am pm	oz./ R min. L		
am pm	oz./ R min. L		
am pm	oz./ R min. L		
am pm	oz./ R min. L		
am pm	oz./ R min. L		
am pm	oz./ R min. L		
am pm	oz./ R min. L		

To Do

Naps

start	finish

Notes

Naps

start	finish

Notes

Reminders

twin tracker

TODAY IS:

| Baby A | | | |

Baby A

Time	Breast/Bottle	Diaper	Meds
am pm	oz./ R min. L		
am pm	oz./ R min. L		
am pm	oz./ R min. L		
am pm	oz./ R min. L		
am pm	oz./ R min. L		
am pm	oz./ R min. L		
am pm	oz./ R min. L		
am pm	oz./ R min. L		

Baby B

Time	Breast/Bottle	Diaper	Meds
am pm	oz./ R min. L		
am pm	oz./ R min. L		
am pm	oz./ R min. L		
am pm	oz./ R min. L		
am pm	oz./ R min. L		
am pm	oz./ R min. L		
am pm	oz./ R min. L		
am pm	oz./ R min. L		

To Do

Naps (Baby A)

start	finish	Notes
		_____
		_____
		_____
		_____
		_____

Naps (Baby B)

start	finish	Notes
		_____
		_____
		_____
		_____
		_____

Reminders

_____
_____
_____
_____
_____
_____
_____
_____

twin tracker

TODAY IS:

Baby A

Time	Breast/Bottle	Diaper	Meds
am pm	oz./ R min. L		
am pm	oz./ R min. L		
am pm	oz./ R min. L		
am pm	oz./ R min. L		
am pm	oz./ R min. L		
am pm	oz./ R min. L		
am pm	oz./ R min. L		
am pm	oz./ R min. L		

Baby B

Time	Breast/Bottle	Diaper	Meds
am pm	oz./ R min. L		
am pm	oz./ R min. L		
am pm	oz./ R min. L		
am pm	oz./ R min. L		
am pm	oz./ R min. L		
am pm	oz./ R min. L		
am pm	oz./ R min. L		
am pm	oz./ R min. L		

To Do

Naps

start	finish

Notes

_____
_____
_____
_____
_____
_____
_____

Naps

start	finish

Notes

_____
_____
_____
_____
_____
_____
_____

Reminders

_____
_____
_____
_____
_____
_____
_____
_____

twin tracker

TODAY IS:

Baby A

Time		Breast/Bottle	Diaper	Meds
am pm		oz./ R min. L		
am pm		oz./ R min. L		
am pm		oz./ R min. L		
am pm		oz./ R min. L		
am pm		oz./ R min. L		
am pm		oz./ R min. L		
am pm		oz./ R min. L		
am pm		oz./ R min. L		

Baby B

Time		Breast/Bottle	Diaper	Meds
am pm		oz./ R min. L		
am pm		oz./ R min. L		
am pm		oz./ R min. L		
am pm		oz./ R min. L		
am pm		oz./ R min. L		
am pm		oz./ R min. L		
am pm		oz./ R min. L		
am pm		oz./ R min. L		

To Do

Naps

start	finish

Notes

Naps

start	finish

Notes

Reminders

twin tracker

TODAY IS:

Baby A

Time	Breast/Bottle	Diaper	Meds
am pm	oz./ R min. L		
am pm	oz./ R min. L		
am pm	oz./ R min. L		
am pm	oz./ R min. L		
am pm	oz./ R min. L		
am pm	oz./ R min. L		
am pm	oz./ R min. L		
am pm	oz./ R min. L		

Baby B

Time	Breast/Bottle	Diaper	Meds
am pm	oz./ R min. L		
am pm	oz./ R min. L		
am pm	oz./ R min. L		
am pm	oz./ R min. L		
am pm	oz./ R min. L		
am pm	oz./ R min. L		
am pm	oz./ R min. L		
am pm	oz./ R min. L		

To Do

Naps

start	finish

Notes

_____

_____

_____

_____

_____

Naps

start	finish

Notes

_____

_____

_____

_____

_____

Reminders

_____

_____

_____

_____

_____

_____

_____

twin tracker

TODAY IS:

Baby A

Time		Breast/Bottle	Diaper	Meds
am pm		oz./ R min. L		
am pm		oz./ R min. L		
am pm		oz./ R min. L		
am pm		oz./ R min. L		
am pm		oz./ R min. L		
am pm		oz./ R min. L		
am pm		oz./ R min. L		
am pm		oz./ R min. L		

Baby B

Time		Breast/Bottle	Diaper	Meds
am pm		oz./ R min. L		
am pm		oz./ R min. L		
am pm		oz./ R min. L		
am pm		oz./ R min. L		
am pm		oz./ R min. L		
am pm		oz./ R min. L		
am pm		oz./ R min. L		
am pm		oz./ R min. L		

To Do

Naps

start	finish

Notes

Naps

start	finish

Notes

Reminders

twin tracker

TODAY IS:

Baby A

Time	Breast/Bottle	Diaper	Meds
am pm	oz./ R min. L		
am pm	oz./ R min. L		
am pm	oz./ R min. L		
am pm	oz./ R min. L		
am pm	oz./ R min. L		
am pm	oz./ R min. L		
am pm	oz./ R min. L		
am pm	oz./ R min. L		

Baby B

Time	Breast/Bottle	Diaper	Meds
am pm	oz./ R min. L		
am pm	oz./ R min. L		
am pm	oz./ R min. L		
am pm	oz./ R min. L		
am pm	oz./ R min. L		
am pm	oz./ R min. L		
am pm	oz./ R min. L		
am pm	oz./ R min. L		

To Do

Naps

start	finish	Notes

Naps

start	finish	Notes

Reminders

twin tracker

TODAY IS:

Baby A

Time	Breast/Bottle	Diaper	Meds
am pm	oz./ R min. L		
am pm	oz./ R min. L		
am pm	oz./ R min. L		
am pm	oz./ R min. L		
am pm	oz./ R min. L		
am pm	oz./ R min. L		
am pm	oz./ R min. L		
am pm	oz./ R min. L		

Baby B

Time	Breast/Bottle	Diaper	Meds
am pm	oz./ R min. L		
am pm	oz./ R min. L		
am pm	oz./ R min. L		
am pm	oz./ R min. L		
am pm	oz./ R min. L		
am pm	oz./ R min. L		
am pm	oz./ R min. L		
am pm	oz./ R min. L		

To Do

Naps

start	finish

Notes

Naps

start	finish

Notes

Reminders

twin tracker

TODAY IS:

Baby A

Time	Breast/Bottle	Diaper	Meds
am pm	oz./ R min. L		
am pm	oz./ R min. L		
am pm	oz./ R min. L		
am pm	oz./ R min. L		
am pm	oz./ R min. L		
am pm	oz./ R min. L		
am pm	oz./ R min. L		
am pm	oz./ R min. L		

Baby B

Time	Breast/Bottle	Diaper	Meds
am pm	oz./ R min. L		
am pm	oz./ R min. L		
am pm	oz./ R min. L		
am pm	oz./ R min. L		
am pm	oz./ R min. L		
am pm	oz./ R min. L		
am pm	oz./ R min. L		
am pm	oz./ R min. L		

To Do

Naps

start	finish

Notes

_____
_____
_____
_____
_____

Naps

start	finish

Notes

_____
_____
_____
_____
_____

Reminders

_____
_____
_____
_____
_____
_____
_____
_____

twin tracker

TODAY IS:

Baby A

Time		Breast/Bottle	Diaper	Meds
am	pm	oz./ R min. L		
am	pm	oz./ R min. L		
am	pm	oz./ R min. L		
am	pm	oz./ R min. L		
am	pm	oz./ R min. L		
am	pm	oz./ R min. L		
am	pm	oz./ R min. L		
am	pm	oz./ R min. L		

Baby B

Time		Breast/Bottle	Diaper	Meds
am	pm	oz./ R min. L		
am	pm	oz./ R min. L		
am	pm	oz./ R min. L		
am	pm	oz./ R min. L		
am	pm	oz./ R min. L		
am	pm	oz./ R min. L		
am	pm	oz./ R min. L		
am	pm	oz./ R min. L		

To Do

Naps

start	finish

Notes

_____
_____
_____
_____
_____

Naps

start	finish

Notes

_____
_____
_____
_____
_____

Reminders

_____
_____
_____
_____
_____
_____
_____
_____

twin tracker

TODAY IS:

Baby A

Time	Breast/Bottle	Diaper	Meds
am pm	oz./ R min. L		
am pm	oz./ R min. L		
am pm	oz./ R min. L		
am pm	oz./ R min. L		
am pm	oz./ R min. L		
am pm	oz./ R min. L		
am pm	oz./ R min. L		
am pm	oz./ R min. L		

Baby B

Time	Breast/Bottle	Diaper	Meds
am pm	oz./ R min. L		
am pm	oz./ R min. L		
am pm	oz./ R min. L		
am pm	oz./ R min. L		
am pm	oz./ R min. L		
am pm	oz./ R min. L		
am pm	oz./ R min. L		
am pm	oz./ R min. L		

To Do

Naps

start	finish

Notes

Naps

start	finish

Notes

Reminders

twin tracker

TODAY IS:

Baby A

Time		Breast/Bottle	Diaper	Meds
am	pm	oz./ R min. L		
am	pm	oz./ R min. L		
am	pm	oz./ R min. L		
am	pm	oz./ R min. L		
am	pm	oz./ R min. L		
am	pm	oz./ R min. L		
am	pm	oz./ R min. L		
am	pm	oz./ R min. L		

Naps

start	finish

Notes

_____
_____
_____
_____
_____

Baby B

Time		Breast/Bottle	Diaper	Meds
am	pm	oz./ R min. L		
am	pm	oz./ R min. L		
am	pm	oz./ R min. L		
am	pm	oz./ R min. L		
am	pm	oz./ R min. L		
am	pm	oz./ R min. L		
am	pm	oz./ R min. L		
am	pm	oz./ R min. L		

Naps

start	finish

Notes

_____
_____
_____
_____
_____

To Do

Reminders

_____
_____
_____
_____
_____
_____
_____

twin tracker

TODAY IS:

Baby A

Time	Breast/Bottle	Diaper	Meds
am pm	oz. / R min. L		
am pm	oz. / R min. L		
am pm	oz. / R min. L		
am pm	oz. / R min. L		
am pm	oz. / R min. L		
am pm	oz. / R min. L		
am pm	oz. / R min. L		
am pm	oz. / R min. L		

Baby B

Time	Breast/Bottle	Diaper	Meds
am pm	oz. / R min. L		
am pm	oz. / R min. L		
am pm	oz. / R min. L		
am pm	oz. / R min. L		
am pm	oz. / R min. L		
am pm	oz. / R min. L		
am pm	oz. / R min. L		
am pm	oz. / R min. L		

To Do

Naps

start	finish

Notes

_____
_____
_____
_____
_____
_____

Naps

start	finish

Notes

_____
_____
_____
_____
_____
_____

Reminders

_____
_____
_____
_____
_____
_____
_____
_____

twin tracker

TODAY IS:

Baby A

Time	Breast/Bottle	Diaper	Meds
am pm	oz./ R min. L		
am pm	oz./ R min. L		
am pm	oz./ R min. L		
am pm	oz./ R min. L		
am pm	oz./ R min. L		
am pm	oz./ R min. L		
am pm	oz./ R min. L		
am pm	oz./ R min. L		

Naps

start	finish

Notes

_____
_____
_____
_____
_____

Baby B

Time	Breast/Bottle	Diaper	Meds
am pm	oz./ R min. L		
am pm	oz./ R min. L		
am pm	oz./ R min. L		
am pm	oz./ R min. L		
am pm	oz./ R min. L		
am pm	oz./ R min. L		
am pm	oz./ R min. L		
am pm	oz./ R min. L		

Naps

start	finish

Notes

_____
_____
_____
_____
_____

To Do

Reminders

_____
_____
_____
_____
_____
_____
_____
_____

twin tracker

TODAY IS:

Baby A

Time	Breast/Bottle	Diaper	Meds
am pm	oz./ R min. L		
am pm	oz./ R min. L		
am pm	oz./ R min. L		
am pm	oz./ R min. L		
am pm	oz./ R min. L		
am pm	oz./ R min. L		
am pm	oz./ R min. L		
am pm	oz./ R min. L		

Naps

start	finish

Notes

_____
_____
_____
_____
_____
_____
_____

Baby B

Time	Breast/Bottle	Diaper	Meds
am pm	oz./ R min. L		
am pm	oz./ R min. L		
am pm	oz./ R min. L		
am pm	oz./ R min. L		
am pm	oz./ R min. L		
am pm	oz./ R min. L		
am pm	oz./ R min. L		
am pm	oz./ R min. L		

Naps

start	finish

Notes

_____
_____
_____
_____
_____
_____
_____

To Do

Reminders

_____
_____
_____
_____
_____
_____
_____

twin tracker

TODAY IS:

Baby A

Time	Breast/Bottle	Diaper	Meds
am pm	oz./ R min. L		
am pm	oz./ R min. L		
am pm	oz./ R min. L		
am pm	oz./ R min. L		
am pm	oz./ R min. L		
am pm	oz./ R min. L		
am pm	oz./ R min. L		
am pm	oz./ R min. L		

Baby B

Time	Breast/Bottle	Diaper	Meds
am pm	oz./ R min. L		
am pm	oz./ R min. L		
am pm	oz./ R min. L		
am pm	oz./ R min. L		
am pm	oz./ R min. L		
am pm	oz./ R min. L		
am pm	oz./ R min. L		
am pm	oz./ R min. L		

To Do

Naps (Baby A)

start	finish	Notes

Naps (Baby B)

start	finish	Notes

Reminders

twin tracker

TODAY IS:

Baby A

Time	Breast/Bottle	Diaper	Meds
am pm	oz./ R min. L		
am pm	oz./ R min. L		
am pm	oz./ R min. L		
am pm	oz./ R min. L		
am pm	oz./ R min. L		
am pm	oz./ R min. L		
am pm	oz./ R min. L		
am pm	oz./ R min. L		

Baby B

Time	Breast/Bottle	Diaper	Meds
am pm	oz./ R min. L		
am pm	oz./ R min. L		
am pm	oz./ R min. L		
am pm	oz./ R min. L		
am pm	oz./ R min. L		
am pm	oz./ R min. L		
am pm	oz./ R min. L		
am pm	oz./ R min. L		

To Do

Naps

start	finish

Notes

_____
_____
_____
_____
_____

Naps

start	finish

Notes

_____
_____
_____
_____
_____

Reminders

_____
_____
_____
_____
_____
_____
_____

twin tracker

TODO IS:

Baby A

Time	Breast/Bottle	Diaper	Meds
am pm	oz./ R min. L		
am pm	oz./ R min. L		
am pm	oz./ R min. L		
am pm	oz./ R min. L		
am pm	oz./ R min. L		
am pm	oz./ R min. L		
am pm	oz./ R min. L		
am pm	oz./ R min. L		

Baby B

Time	Breast/Bottle	Diaper	Meds
am pm	oz./ R min. L		
am pm	oz./ R min. L		
am pm	oz./ R min. L		
am pm	oz./ R min. L		
am pm	oz./ R min. L		
am pm	oz./ R min. L		
am pm	oz./ R min. L		
am pm	oz./ R min. L		

To Do

Naps

start	finish

Notes

_____
_____
_____
_____
_____

Naps

start	finish

Notes

_____
_____
_____
_____
_____

Reminders

_____
_____
_____
_____
_____
_____
_____
_____

twin tracker

TODAY IS:

Baby A

Time	Breast/Bottle	Diaper	Meds
am pm	oz./ R min. L		
am pm	oz./ R min. L		
am pm	oz./ R min. L		
am pm	oz./ R min. L		
am pm	oz./ R min. L		
am pm	oz./ R min. L		
am pm	oz./ R min. L		
am pm	oz./ R min. L		

Baby B

Time	Breast/Bottle	Diaper	Meds
am pm	oz./ R min. L		
am pm	oz./ R min. L		
am pm	oz./ R min. L		
am pm	oz./ R min. L		
am pm	oz./ R min. L		
am pm	oz./ R min. L		
am pm	oz./ R min. L		
am pm	oz./ R min. L		

To Do

Naps

start	finish

Notes
_____
_____
_____
_____
_____

Naps

start	finish

Notes
_____
_____
_____
_____
_____

Reminders

_____
_____
_____
_____
_____
_____
_____
_____

twin tracker

TODAY IS:

Baby A

Time	Breast/Bottle	Diaper	Meds
am pm	oz./ R min. L		
am pm	oz./ R min. L		
am pm	oz./ R min. L		
am pm	oz./ R min. L		
am pm	oz./ R min. L		
am pm	oz./ R min. L		
am pm	oz./ R min. L		
am pm	oz./ R min. L		

Naps

start	finish	Notes
		_____
		_____
		_____
		_____
		_____

Baby B

Time	Breast/Bottle	Diaper	Meds
am pm	oz./ R min. L		
am pm	oz./ R min. L		
am pm	oz./ R min. L		
am pm	oz./ R min. L		
am pm	oz./ R min. L		
am pm	oz./ R min. L		
am pm	oz./ R min. L		
am pm	oz./ R min. L		

Naps

start	finish	Notes
		_____
		_____
		_____
		_____
		_____

To Do

Reminders

_____
_____
_____
_____
_____
_____
_____

twin tracker

TODAY IS:

Baby A

Time	Breast/Bottle	Diaper	Meds
am pm	oz./ R min. L		
am pm	oz./ R min. L		
am pm	oz./ R min. L		
am pm	oz./ R min. L		
am pm	oz./ R min. L		
am pm	oz./ R min. L		
am pm	oz./ R min. L		
am pm	oz./ R min. L		

Naps

start	finish

Notes

_____
_____
_____
_____
_____
_____

Baby B

Time	Breast/Bottle	Diaper	Meds
am pm	oz./ R min. L		
am pm	oz./ R min. L		
am pm	oz./ R min. L		
am pm	oz./ R min. L		
am pm	oz./ R min. L		
am pm	oz./ R min. L		
am pm	oz./ R min. L		
am pm	oz./ R min. L		

Naps

start	finish

Notes

_____
_____
_____
_____
_____
_____

To Do

Reminders

_____
_____
_____
_____
_____
_____
_____
_____

twin tracker

TODO IS:

Baby A

Time	Breast/Bottle	Diaper	Meds
am pm	oz./ R min. L		
am pm	oz./ R min. L		
am pm	oz./ R min. L		
am pm	oz./ R min. L		
am pm	oz./ R min. L		
am pm	oz./ R min. L		
am pm	oz./ R min. L		
am pm	oz./ R min. L		

Baby B

Time	Breast/Bottle	Diaper	Meds
am pm	oz./ R min. L		
am pm	oz./ R min. L		
am pm	oz./ R min. L		
am pm	oz./ R min. L		
am pm	oz./ R min. L		
am pm	oz./ R min. L		
am pm	oz./ R min. L		
am pm	oz./ R min. L		

To Do

Naps

start	finish

Notes

Naps

start	finish

Notes

Reminders

twin tracker

TODAY IS:

Baby A

Time	Breast/ Bottle	Diaper	Meds
am pm	oz./ R min. L		
am pm	oz./ R min. L		
am pm	oz./ R min. L		
am pm	oz./ R min. L		
am pm	oz./ R min. L		
am pm	oz./ R min. L		
am pm	oz./ R min. L		
am pm	oz./ R min. L		

Baby B

Time	Breast/ Bottle	Diaper	Meds
am pm	oz./ R min. L		
am pm	oz./ R min. L		
am pm	oz./ R min. L		
am pm	oz./ R min. L		
am pm	oz./ R min. L		
am pm	oz./ R min. L		
am pm	oz./ R min. L		
am pm	oz./ R min. L		

To Do

Naps

start	finish

Notes

Naps

start	finish

Notes

Reminders

twin tracker

TODAY IS:

Baby A

Time	Breast/Bottle	Diaper	Meds
am pm	oz./ R min. L		
am pm	oz./ R min. L		
am pm	oz./ R min. L		
am pm	oz./ R min. L		
am pm	oz./ R min. L		
am pm	oz./ R min. L		
am pm	oz./ R min. L		
am pm	oz./ R min. L		

Baby B

Time	Breast/Bottle	Diaper	Meds
am pm	oz./ R min. L		
am pm	oz./ R min. L		
am pm	oz./ R min. L		
am pm	oz./ R min. L		
am pm	oz./ R min. L		
am pm	oz./ R min. L		
am pm	oz./ R min. L		
am pm	oz./ R min. L		

To Do

Naps

start	finish

Notes

Naps

start	finish

Notes

Reminders

twin tracker

TODAY IS:

Baby A

Time	Breast/Bottle	Diaper	Meds
am pm	oz./ R min. L		
am pm	oz./ R min. L		
am pm	oz./ R min. L		
am pm	oz./ R min. L		
am pm	oz./ R min. L		
am pm	oz./ R min. L		
am pm	oz./ R min. L		
am pm	oz./ R min. L		

Baby B

Time	Breast/Bottle	Diaper	Meds
am pm	oz./ R min. L		
am pm	oz./ R min. L		
am pm	oz./ R min. L		
am pm	oz./ R min. L		
am pm	oz./ R min. L		
am pm	oz./ R min. L		
am pm	oz./ R min. L		
am pm	oz./ R min. L		

To Do

Naps (Baby A)

start	finish

Notes

Naps (Baby B)

start	finish

Notes

Reminders

twin tracker

TODAY IS:

Baby A

Time		Breast/Bottle	Diaper	Meds
am pm		oz./ R min. L		
am pm		oz./ R min. L		
am pm		oz./ R min. L		
am pm		oz./ R min. L		
am pm		oz./ R min. L		
am pm		oz./ R min. L		
am pm		oz./ R min. L		
am pm		oz./ R min. L		

Baby B

Time		Breast/Bottle	Diaper	Meds
am pm		oz./ R min. L		
am pm		oz./ R min. L		
am pm		oz./ R min. L		
am pm		oz./ R min. L		
am pm		oz./ R min. L		
am pm		oz./ R min. L		
am pm		oz./ R min. L		
am pm		oz./ R min. L		

To Do

Naps

start	finish

Notes

Naps

start	finish

Notes

Reminders

twin tracker

TODAY IS:

Baby A

Time	Breast/Bottle	Diaper	Meds
am pm	oz./ R min. L		
am pm	oz./ R min. L		
am pm	oz./ R min. L		
am pm	oz./ R min. L		
am pm	oz./ R min. L		
am pm	oz./ R min. L		
am pm	oz./ R min. L		
am pm	oz./ R min. L		

Baby B

Time	Breast/Bottle	Diaper	Meds
am pm	oz./ R min. L		
am pm	oz./ R min. L		
am pm	oz./ R min. L		
am pm	oz./ R min. L		
am pm	oz./ R min. L		
am pm	oz./ R min. L		
am pm	oz./ R min. L		
am pm	oz./ R min. L		

To Do

Naps

start	finish

Notes

_____
_____
_____
_____
_____
_____

Naps

start	finish

Notes

_____
_____
_____
_____
_____
_____

Reminders

_____
_____
_____
_____
_____
_____
_____
_____

twin tracker

TODAY IS:

Baby A

Time	Breast/Bottle	Diaper	Meds
am pm	oz./ R min. L		
am pm	oz./ R min. L		
am pm	oz./ R min. L		
am pm	oz./ R min. L		
am pm	oz./ R min. L		
am pm	oz./ R min. L		
am pm	oz./ R min. L		
am pm	oz./ R min. L		

Naps

start	finish

Notes

_____
_____
_____
_____
_____

Baby B

Time	Breast/Bottle	Diaper	Meds
am pm	oz./ R min. L		
am pm	oz./ R min. L		
am pm	oz./ R min. L		
am pm	oz./ R min. L		
am pm	oz./ R min. L		
am pm	oz./ R min. L		
am pm	oz./ R min. L		
am pm	oz./ R min. L		

Naps

start	finish

Notes

_____
_____
_____
_____
_____

To Do

Reminders

_____
_____
_____
_____
_____
_____
_____

twin tracker

TODAY IS:

Baby A

Time	Breast/Bottle	Diaper	Meds
am pm	oz./ R min. L		
am pm	oz./ R min. L		
am pm	oz./ R min. L		
am pm	oz./ R min. L		
am pm	oz./ R min. L		
am pm	oz./ R min. L		
am pm	oz./ R min. L		
am pm	oz./ R min. L		

Baby B

Time	Breast/Bottle	Diaper	Meds
am pm	oz./ R min. L		
am pm	oz./ R min. L		
am pm	oz./ R min. L		
am pm	oz./ R min. L		
am pm	oz./ R min. L		
am pm	oz./ R min. L		
am pm	oz./ R min. L		
am pm	oz./ R min. L		

To Do

Naps

start	finish

Notes

_____
_____
_____
_____
_____
_____

Naps

start	finish

Notes

_____
_____
_____
_____
_____
_____

Reminders

_____
_____
_____
_____
_____
_____
_____
_____

twin tracker

TODAY IS:

Baby A

Time	Breast/Bottle	Diaper	Meds
am pm	oz./ R min. L		
am pm	oz./ R min. L		
am pm	oz./ R min. L		
am pm	oz./ R min. L		
am pm	oz./ R min. L		
am pm	oz./ R min. L		
am pm	oz./ R min. L		
am pm	oz./ R min. L		

Baby B

Time	Breast/Bottle	Diaper	Meds
am pm	oz./ R min. L		
am pm	oz./ R min. L		
am pm	oz./ R min. L		
am pm	oz./ R min. L		
am pm	oz./ R min. L		
am pm	oz./ R min. L		
am pm	oz./ R min. L		
am pm	oz./ R min. L		

To Do

Naps

start	finish

Notes

Naps

start	finish

Notes

Reminders

twin tracker

TODAY IS:

Baby A

Time	Breast/Bottle	Diaper	Meds
am pm	oz./ R min. L		
am pm	oz./ R min. L		
am pm	oz./ R min. L		
am pm	oz./ R min. L		
am pm	oz./ R min. L		
am pm	oz./ R min. L		
am pm	oz./ R min. L		
am pm	oz./ R min. L		

Naps

start	finish

Notes

_____
_____
_____
_____
_____
_____

Baby B

Time	Breast/Bottle	Diaper	Meds
am pm	oz./ R min. L		
am pm	oz./ R min. L		
am pm	oz./ R min. L		
am pm	oz./ R min. L		
am pm	oz./ R min. L		
am pm	oz./ R min. L		
am pm	oz./ R min. L		
am pm	oz./ R min. L		

Naps

start	finish

Notes

_____
_____
_____
_____
_____
_____

To Do

Reminders

_____
_____
_____
_____
_____
_____
_____
_____

twin tracker

TODAY IS:

Baby A

Time		Breast/Bottle	Diaper	Meds
am pm		oz./ R min. L		
am pm		oz./ R min. L		
am pm		oz./ R min. L		
am pm		oz./ R min. L		
am pm		oz./ R min. L		
am pm		oz./ R min. L		
am pm		oz./ R min. L		
am pm		oz./ R min. L		

Baby B

Time		Breast/Bottle	Diaper	Meds
am pm		oz./ R min. L		
am pm		oz./ R min. L		
am pm		oz./ R min. L		
am pm		oz./ R min. L		
am pm		oz./ R min. L		
am pm		oz./ R min. L		
am pm		oz./ R min. L		
am pm		oz./ R min. L		

To Do

Naps

start	finish

Notes

Naps

start	finish

Notes

Reminders

twin tracker

TODAY IS:

Baby A

Time	Breast/Bottle	Diaper	Meds
am pm	oz./ R min. L		
am pm	oz./ R min. L		
am pm	oz./ R min. L		
am pm	oz./ R min. L		
am pm	oz./ R min. L		
am pm	oz./ R min. L		
am pm	oz./ R min. L		
am pm	oz./ R min. L		

Baby B

Time	Breast/Bottle	Diaper	Meds
am pm	oz./ R min. L		
am pm	oz./ R min. L		
am pm	oz./ R min. L		
am pm	oz./ R min. L		
am pm	oz./ R min. L		
am pm	oz./ R min. L		
am pm	oz./ R min. L		
am pm	oz./ R min. L		

To Do

Reminders

Naps

start	finish

Notes

Naps

start	finish

Notes

twin tracker

TODAY IS:

Baby A

Time	Breast/Bottle	Diaper	Meds
am pm	oz./ R min. L		
am pm	oz./ R min. L		
am pm	oz./ R min. L		
am pm	oz./ R min. L		
am pm	oz./ R min. L		
am pm	oz./ R min. L		
am pm	oz./ R min. L		
am pm	oz./ R min. L		

Baby B

Time	Breast/Bottle	Diaper	Meds
am pm	oz./ R min. L		
am pm	oz./ R min. L		
am pm	oz./ R min. L		
am pm	oz./ R min. L		
am pm	oz./ R min. L		
am pm	oz./ R min. L		
am pm	oz./ R min. L		
am pm	oz./ R min. L		

To Do

Naps

start	finish

Notes

Naps

start	finish

Notes

Reminders

twin tracker

TODAY IS:

Baby A

Time	Breast/Bottle	Diaper	Meds
am pm	oz./ R min. L		
am pm	oz./ R min. L		
am pm	oz./ R min. L		
am pm	oz./ R min. L		
am pm	oz./ R min. L		
am pm	oz./ R min. L		
am pm	oz./ R min. L		
am pm	oz./ R min. L		

Baby B

Time	Breast/Bottle	Diaper	Meds
am pm	oz./ R min. L		
am pm	oz./ R min. L		
am pm	oz./ R min. L		
am pm	oz./ R min. L		
am pm	oz./ R min. L		
am pm	oz./ R min. L		
am pm	oz./ R min. L		
am pm	oz./ R min. L		

To Do

Naps

start	finish

Notes

_____

_____

_____

_____

_____

Naps

start	finish

Notes

_____

_____

_____

_____

_____

Reminders

twin tracker

TODAY IS:

Baby A

Time	Breast/Bottle	Diaper	Meds
am pm	oz./ R min. L		
am pm	oz./ R min. L		
am pm	oz./ R min. L		
am pm	oz./ R min. L		
am pm	oz./ R min. L		
am pm	oz./ R min. L		
am pm	oz./ R min. L		
am pm	oz./ R min. L		

Baby B

Time	Breast/Bottle	Diaper	Meds
am pm	oz./ R min. L		
am pm	oz./ R min. L		
am pm	oz./ R min. L		
am pm	oz./ R min. L		
am pm	oz./ R min. L		
am pm	oz./ R min. L		
am pm	oz./ R min. L		
am pm	oz./ R min. L		

To Do

Naps

start	finish

Notes

_____
_____
_____
_____
_____

Naps

start	finish

Notes

_____
_____
_____
_____
_____

Reminders

_____
_____
_____
_____
_____
_____
_____
_____

twin tracker

TODAY IS:

Baby A

Time	Breast/Bottle	Diaper	Meds
am pm	oz./ R min. L		
am pm	oz./ R min. L		
am pm	oz./ R min. L		
am pm	oz./ R min. L		
am pm	oz./ R min. L		
am pm	oz./ R min. L		
am pm	oz./ R min. L		
am pm	oz./ R min. L		

Baby B

Time	Breast/Bottle	Diaper	Meds
am pm	oz./ R min. L		
am pm	oz./ R min. L		
am pm	oz./ R min. L		
am pm	oz./ R min. L		
am pm	oz./ R min. L		
am pm	oz./ R min. L		
am pm	oz./ R min. L		
am pm	oz./ R min. L		

To Do

Naps

start	finish

Notes

Naps

start	finish

Notes

Reminders

twin tracker

TODAY IS:

Baby A

Time	Breast/Bottle	Diaper	Meds
am pm	oz./ R min. L		
am pm	oz./ R min. L		
am pm	oz./ R min. L		
am pm	oz./ R min. L		
am pm	oz./ R min. L		
am pm	oz./ R min. L		
am pm	oz./ R min. L		
am pm	oz./ R min. L		

Baby B

Time	Breast/Bottle	Diaper	Meds
am pm	oz./ R min. L		
am pm	oz./ R min. L		
am pm	oz./ R min. L		
am pm	oz./ R min. L		
am pm	oz./ R min. L		
am pm	oz./ R min. L		
am pm	oz./ R min. L		
am pm	oz./ R min. L		

To Do

Naps

start	finish

Notes

Naps

start	finish

Notes

Reminders

twin tracker

TODAY IS:

Baby A

Time	Breast/Bottle	Diaper	Meds
am pm	oz./ R min. L		
am pm	oz./ R min. L		
am pm	oz./ R min. L		
am pm	oz./ R min. L		
am pm	oz./ R min. L		
am pm	oz./ R min. L		
am pm	oz./ R min. L		
am pm	oz./ R min. L		

Baby B

Time	Breast/Bottle	Diaper	Meds
am pm	oz./ R min. L		
am pm	oz./ R min. L		
am pm	oz./ R min. L		
am pm	oz./ R min. L		
am pm	oz./ R min. L		
am pm	oz./ R min. L		
am pm	oz./ R min. L		
am pm	oz./ R min. L		

To Do

Naps

start	finish

Notes

_____
_____
_____
_____
_____
_____

Naps

start	finish

Notes

_____
_____
_____
_____
_____
_____

Reminders

_____
_____
_____
_____
_____
_____
_____
_____

twin tracker

TODAY IS:

Baby A

Time	Breast/ Bottle	Diaper	Meds
am pm	oz./ R min. L		
am pm	oz./ R min. L		
am pm	oz./ R min. L		
am pm	oz./ R min. L		
am pm	oz./ R min. L		
am pm	oz./ R min. L		
am pm	oz./ R min. L		
am pm	oz./ R min. L		

Baby B

Time	Breast/ Bottle	Diaper	Meds
am pm	oz./ R min. L		
am pm	oz./ R min. L		
am pm	oz./ R min. L		
am pm	oz./ R min. L		
am pm	oz./ R min. L		
am pm	oz./ R min. L		
am pm	oz./ R min. L		
am pm	oz./ R min. L		

To Do

Naps

start	finish

Notes

_____
_____
_____
_____
_____

Naps

start	finish

Notes

_____
_____
_____
_____
_____

Reminders

_____
_____
_____
_____
_____
_____
_____

twin tracker

TODAY IS:

Baby A

Time	Breast/Bottle	Diaper	Meds
am pm	oz./ R min. L		
am pm	oz./ R min. L		
am pm	oz./ R min. L		
am pm	oz./ R min. L		
am pm	oz./ R min. L		
am pm	oz./ R min. L		
am pm	oz./ R min. L		
am pm	oz./ R min. L		

Baby B

Time	Breast/Bottle	Diaper	Meds
am pm	oz./ R min. L		
am pm	oz./ R min. L		
am pm	oz./ R min. L		
am pm	oz./ R min. L		
am pm	oz./ R min. L		
am pm	oz./ R min. L		
am pm	oz./ R min. L		
am pm	oz./ R min. L		

To Do

Naps

start	finish

Notes

_____
_____
_____
_____
_____
_____

Naps

start	finish

Notes

_____
_____
_____
_____
_____
_____

Reminders

_____
_____
_____
_____
_____
_____
_____
_____

twin tracker

TODAY IS:

Baby A

Time	Breast/Bottle	Diaper	Meds
am pm	oz./ R min. L		
am pm	oz./ R min. L		
am pm	oz./ R min. L		
am pm	oz./ R min. L		
am pm	oz./ R min. L		
am pm	oz./ R min. L		
am pm	oz./ R min. L		
am pm	oz./ R min. L		

Baby B

Time	Breast/Bottle	Diaper	Meds
am pm	oz./ R min. L		
am pm	oz./ R min. L		
am pm	oz./ R min. L		
am pm	oz./ R min. L		
am pm	oz./ R min. L		
am pm	oz./ R min. L		
am pm	oz./ R min. L		
am pm	oz./ R min. L		

To Do

Naps (Baby A)

start	finish

Notes

Naps (Baby B)

start	finish

Notes

Reminders

twin tracker

TODAY IS:

Baby A

Time	Breast/Bottle	Diaper	Meds
am pm	oz./ R min. L		
am pm	oz./ R min. L		
am pm	oz./ R min. L		
am pm	oz./ R min. L		
am pm	oz./ R min. L		
am pm	oz./ R min. L		
am pm	oz./ R min. L		
am pm	oz./ R min. L		

Baby B

Time	Breast/Bottle	Diaper	Meds
am pm	oz./ R min. L		
am pm	oz./ R min. L		
am pm	oz./ R min. L		
am pm	oz./ R min. L		
am pm	oz./ R min. L		
am pm	oz./ R min. L		
am pm	oz./ R min. L		
am pm	oz./ R min. L		

To Do

Naps

start	finish

Notes

_____
_____
_____
_____
_____
_____

Naps

start	finish

Notes

_____
_____
_____
_____
_____
_____

Reminders

_____
_____
_____
_____
_____
_____
_____

twin tracker

TODAY IS:

Baby A

Time	Breast/Bottle	Diaper	Meds
am pm	oz./ R min. L		
am pm	oz./ R min. L		
am pm	oz./ R min. L		
am pm	oz./ R min. L		
am pm	oz./ R min. L		
am pm	oz./ R min. L		
am pm	oz./ R min. L		
am pm	oz./ R min. L		

Naps

start	finish

Notes

_____
_____
_____
_____
_____

Baby B

Time	Breast/Bottle	Diaper	Meds
am pm	oz./ R min. L		
am pm	oz./ R min. L		
am pm	oz./ R min. L		
am pm	oz./ R min. L		
am pm	oz./ R min. L		
am pm	oz./ R min. L		
am pm	oz./ R min. L		
am pm	oz./ R min. L		

Naps

start	finish

Notes

_____
_____
_____
_____
_____

To Do

Reminders

_____
_____
_____
_____
_____
_____
_____
_____

twin tracker

TODAY IS:

Baby A

Time	Breast/Bottle	Diaper	Meds
am pm	oz./ R min. L		
am pm	oz./ R min. L		
am pm	oz./ R min. L		
am pm	oz./ R min. L		
am pm	oz./ R min. L		
am pm	oz./ R min. L		
am pm	oz./ R min. L		
am pm	oz./ R min. L		

Baby B

Time	Breast/Bottle	Diaper	Meds
am pm	oz./ R min. L		
am pm	oz./ R min. L		
am pm	oz./ R min. L		
am pm	oz./ R min. L		
am pm	oz./ R min. L		
am pm	oz./ R min. L		
am pm	oz./ R min. L		
am pm	oz./ R min. L		

To Do

Naps (Baby A)

start	finish

Notes

Naps (Baby B)

start	finish

Notes

Reminders

twin tracker

TODAY IS:

Baby A

Time	Breast/Bottle	Diaper	Meds
am pm	oz./ R min. L		
am pm	oz./ R min. L		
am pm	oz./ R min. L		
am pm	oz./ R min. L		
am pm	oz./ R min. L		
am pm	oz./ R min. L		
am pm	oz./ R min. L		
am pm	oz./ R min. L		

Naps

start	finish

Notes

_____
_____
_____
_____
_____

Baby B

Time	Breast/Bottle	Diaper	Meds
am pm	oz./ R min. L		
am pm	oz./ R min. L		
am pm	oz./ R min. L		
am pm	oz./ R min. L		
am pm	oz./ R min. L		
am pm	oz./ R min. L		
am pm	oz./ R min. L		
am pm	oz./ R min. L		

Naps

start	finish

Notes

_____
_____
_____
_____
_____

To Do

Reminders

_____
_____
_____
_____
_____
_____
_____

twin tracker

TODAY IS:

Baby A

Time	Breast/Bottle	Diaper	Meds
am pm	oz./ R min. L		
am pm	oz./ R min. L		
am pm	oz./ R min. L		
am pm	oz./ R min. L		
am pm	oz./ R min. L		
am pm	oz./ R min. L		
am pm	oz./ R min. L		
am pm	oz./ R min. L		

Baby B

Time	Breast/Bottle	Diaper	Meds
am pm	oz./ R min. L		
am pm	oz./ R min. L		
am pm	oz./ R min. L		
am pm	oz./ R min. L		
am pm	oz./ R min. L		
am pm	oz./ R min. L		
am pm	oz./ R min. L		
am pm	oz./ R min. L		

To Do

Naps

start	finish

Notes

_____
_____
_____
_____
_____
_____

Naps

start	finish

Notes

_____
_____
_____
_____
_____
_____

Reminders

_____
_____
_____
_____
_____
_____
_____

twin tracker

TODAY IS:

Baby A

Time	Breast/Bottle	Diaper	Meds
am pm	oz./ R min. L		
am pm	oz./ R min. L		
am pm	oz./ R min. L		
am pm	oz./ R min. L		
am pm	oz./ R min. L		
am pm	oz./ R min. L		
am pm	oz./ R min. L		
am pm	oz./ R min. L		

Baby B

Time	Breast/Bottle	Diaper	Meds
am pm	oz./ R min. L		
am pm	oz./ R min. L		
am pm	oz./ R min. L		
am pm	oz./ R min. L		
am pm	oz./ R min. L		
am pm	oz./ R min. L		
am pm	oz./ R min. L		
am pm	oz./ R min. L		

To Do

Naps

start	finish

Notes

Naps

start	finish

Notes

Reminders

twin tracker

TODAY IS:

Baby A

Time	Breast/ Bottle	Diaper	Meds
am pm	oz./ R min. L		
am pm	oz./ R min. L		
am pm	oz./ R min. L		
am pm	oz./ R min. L		
am pm	oz./ R min. L		
am pm	oz./ R min. L		
am pm	oz./ R min. L		
am pm	oz./ R min. L		

Naps

start	finish

Notes

_____
_____
_____
_____
_____
_____

Baby B

Time	Breast/ Bottle	Diaper	Meds
am pm	oz./ R min. L		
am pm	oz./ R min. L		
am pm	oz./ R min. L		
am pm	oz./ R min. L		
am pm	oz./ R min. L		
am pm	oz./ R min. L		
am pm	oz./ R min. L		
am pm	oz./ R min. L		

Naps

start	finish

Notes

_____
_____
_____
_____
_____
_____

To Do

Reminders

_____
_____
_____
_____
_____
_____
_____
_____

twin tracker

TODAY IS:

Baby A

Time	Breast/Bottle	Diaper	Meds
am pm	oz./ R min. L		
am pm	oz./ R min. L		
am pm	oz./ R min. L		
am pm	oz./ R min. L		
am pm	oz./ R min. L		
am pm	oz./ R min. L		
am pm	oz./ R min. L		
am pm	oz./ R min. L		

Baby B

Time	Breast/Bottle	Diaper	Meds
am pm	oz./ R min. L		
am pm	oz./ R min. L		
am pm	oz./ R min. L		
am pm	oz./ R min. L		
am pm	oz./ R min. L		
am pm	oz./ R min. L		
am pm	oz./ R min. L		
am pm	oz./ R min. L		

To Do

Naps

start	finish

Notes

Naps

start	finish

Notes

Reminders

twin tracker

TODAY IS:

Baby A

Time	Breast/Bottle	Diaper	Meds
am pm	oz./ R min. L		
am pm	oz./ R min. L		
am pm	oz./ R min. L		
am pm	oz./ R min. L		
am pm	oz./ R min. L		
am pm	oz./ R min. L		
am pm	oz./ R min. L		
am pm	oz./ R min. L		

Naps

start	finish

Notes

_____
_____
_____
_____
_____
_____

Baby B

Time	Breast/Bottle	Diaper	Meds
am pm	oz./ R min. L		
am pm	oz./ R min. L		
am pm	oz./ R min. L		
am pm	oz./ R min. L		
am pm	oz./ R min. L		
am pm	oz./ R min. L		
am pm	oz./ R min. L		
am pm	oz./ R min. L		

Naps

start	finish

Notes

_____
_____
_____
_____
_____
_____

To Do

Reminders

_____
_____
_____
_____
_____
_____
_____
_____

twin tracker

TODAY IS:

Baby A

Time	Breast/Bottle	Diaper	Meds
am pm	oz./ R min. L		
am pm	oz./ R min. L		
am pm	oz./ R min. L		
am pm	oz./ R min. L		
am pm	oz./ R min. L		
am pm	oz./ R min. L		
am pm	oz./ R min. L		
am pm	oz./ R min. L		

Baby B

Time	Breast/Bottle	Diaper	Meds
am pm	oz./ R min. L		
am pm	oz./ R min. L		
am pm	oz./ R min. L		
am pm	oz./ R min. L		
am pm	oz./ R min. L		
am pm	oz./ R min. L		
am pm	oz./ R min. L		
am pm	oz./ R min. L		

To Do

Naps

start	finish

Notes

Naps

start	finish

Notes

Reminders

twin tracker

TODAY IS:

Baby A

Time	Breast/Bottle	Diaper	Meds
am pm	oz./ R min. L		
am pm	oz./ R min. L		
am pm	oz./ R min. L		
am pm	oz./ R min. L		
am pm	oz./ R min. L		
am pm	oz./ R min. L		
am pm	oz./ R min. L		
am pm	oz./ R min. L		

Naps

start	finish

Notes

_____
_____
_____
_____
_____
_____

Baby B

Time	Breast/Bottle	Diaper	Meds
am pm	oz./ R min. L		
am pm	oz./ R min. L		
am pm	oz./ R min. L		
am pm	oz./ R min. L		
am pm	oz./ R min. L		
am pm	oz./ R min. L		
am pm	oz./ R min. L		
am pm	oz./ R min. L		

Naps

start	finish

Notes

_____
_____
_____
_____
_____
_____

To Do

Reminders

_____
_____
_____
_____
_____
_____
_____
_____

twin tracker

TODAY IS:

Baby A

Time	Breast/Bottle	Diaper	Meds
am pm	oz./ R min. L		
am pm	oz./ R min. L		
am pm	oz./ R min. L		
am pm	oz./ R min. L		
am pm	oz./ R min. L		
am pm	oz./ R min. L		
am pm	oz./ R min. L		
am pm	oz./ R min. L		

Naps

start	finish

Notes

_____
_____
_____
_____
_____

Baby B

Time	Breast/Bottle	Diaper	Meds
am pm	oz./ R min. L		
am pm	oz./ R min. L		
am pm	oz./ R min. L		
am pm	oz./ R min. L		
am pm	oz./ R min. L		
am pm	oz./ R min. L		
am pm	oz./ R min. L		
am pm	oz./ R min. L		

Naps

start	finish

Notes

_____
_____
_____
_____
_____

To Do

Reminders

_____
_____
_____
_____
_____
_____
_____

twin tracker

TODAY IS:

Baby A

Time	Breast/Bottle	Diaper	Meds
am pm	oz./ R min. L		
am pm	oz./ R min. L		
am pm	oz./ R min. L		
am pm	oz./ R min. L		
am pm	oz./ R min. L		
am pm	oz./ R min. L		
am pm	oz./ R min. L		
am pm	oz./ R min. L		

Naps

start	finish

Notes

_____
_____
_____
_____
_____
_____
_____

Baby B

Time	Breast/Bottle	Diaper	Meds
am pm	oz./ R min. L		
am pm	oz./ R min. L		
am pm	oz./ R min. L		
am pm	oz./ R min. L		
am pm	oz./ R min. L		
am pm	oz./ R min. L		
am pm	oz./ R min. L		
am pm	oz./ R min. L		

Naps

start	finish

Notes

_____
_____
_____
_____
_____
_____
_____

To Do

Reminders

_____
_____
_____
_____
_____
_____
_____
_____

twin tracker

TODAY IS:

Baby A

Time	Breast/Bottle	Diaper	Meds
am pm	oz./ R min. L		
am pm	oz./ R min. L		
am pm	oz./ R min. L		
am pm	oz./ R min. L		
am pm	oz./ R min. L		
am pm	oz./ R min. L		
am pm	oz./ R min. L		
am pm	oz./ R min. L		

Baby B

Time	Breast/Bottle	Diaper	Meds
am pm	oz./ R min. L		
am pm	oz./ R min. L		
am pm	oz./ R min. L		
am pm	oz./ R min. L		
am pm	oz./ R min. L		
am pm	oz./ R min. L		
am pm	oz./ R min. L		
am pm	oz./ R min. L		

To Do

Naps

start	finish	Notes

Naps

start	finish	Notes

Reminders

twin tracker

TODAY IS:

Baby A

Time	Breast/Bottle	Diaper	Meds
am pm	oz./ R min. L		
am pm	oz./ R min. L		
am pm	oz./ R min. L		
am pm	oz./ R min. L		
am pm	oz./ R min. L		
am pm	oz./ R min. L		
am pm	oz./ R min. L		
am pm	oz./ R min. L		

Naps

start	finish

Notes

_____
_____
_____
_____
_____
_____

Baby B

Time	Breast/Bottle	Diaper	Meds
am pm	oz./ R min. L		
am pm	oz./ R min. L		
am pm	oz./ R min. L		
am pm	oz./ R min. L		
am pm	oz./ R min. L		
am pm	oz./ R min. L		
am pm	oz./ R min. L		
am pm	oz./ R min. L		

Naps

start	finish

Notes

_____
_____
_____
_____
_____
_____

To Do

Reminders

_____
_____
_____
_____
_____
_____
_____
_____

twin tracker

TODAY IS:

Baby A

Time	Breast/ Bottle	Diaper	Meds
am pm	oz./ R min. L		
am pm	oz./ R min. L		
am pm	oz./ R min. L		
am pm	oz./ R min. L		
am pm	oz./ R min. L		
am pm	oz./ R min. L		
am pm	oz./ R min. L		
am pm	oz./ R min. L		

Naps

start	finish	Notes
		_____
		_____
		_____
		_____
		_____

Baby B

Time	Breast/ Bottle	Diaper	Meds
am pm	oz./ R min. L		
am pm	oz./ R min. L		
am pm	oz./ R min. L		
am pm	oz./ R min. L		
am pm	oz./ R min. L		
am pm	oz./ R min. L		
am pm	oz./ R min. L		
am pm	oz./ R min. L		

Naps

start	finish	Notes
		_____
		_____
		_____
		_____
		_____

To Do

Reminders

_____

_____

_____

_____

_____

_____

_____

twin tracker

TODAY IS:

Baby A

Time	Breast/Bottle	Diaper	Meds
am pm	oz./ R min. L		
am pm	oz./ R min. L		
am pm	oz./ R min. L		
am pm	oz./ R min. L		
am pm	oz./ R min. L		
am pm	oz./ R min. L		
am pm	oz./ R min. L		
am pm	oz./ R min. L		

Baby B

Time	Breast/Bottle	Diaper	Meds
am pm	oz./ R min. L		
am pm	oz./ R min. L		
am pm	oz./ R min. L		
am pm	oz./ R min. L		
am pm	oz./ R min. L		
am pm	oz./ R min. L		
am pm	oz./ R min. L		
am pm	oz./ R min. L		

To Do

Naps

start	finish

Notes

_____
_____
_____
_____
_____

Naps

start	finish

Notes

_____
_____
_____
_____
_____

Reminders

_____
_____
_____
_____
_____
_____
_____
_____

twin tracker

TODAY IS:

Baby A

Time	Breast/ Bottle	Diaper	Meds
am pm	oz./ R min. L		
am pm	oz./ R min. L		
am pm	oz./ R min. L		
am pm	oz./ R min. L		
am pm	oz./ R min. L		
am pm	oz./ R min. L		
am pm	oz./ R min. L		
am pm	oz./ R min. L		

Baby B

Time	Breast/ Bottle	Diaper	Meds
am pm	oz./ R min. L		
am pm	oz./ R min. L		
am pm	oz./ R min. L		
am pm	oz./ R min. L		
am pm	oz./ R min. L		
am pm	oz./ R min. L		
am pm	oz./ R min. L		
am pm	oz./ R min. L		

To Do

Naps

start	finish

Notes

_____
_____
_____
_____
_____

Naps

start	finish

Notes

_____
_____
_____
_____
_____

Reminders

_____
_____
_____
_____
_____
_____
_____

twin tracker

TODAY IS:

Baby A

Time	Breast/Bottle	Diaper	Meds
am pm	oz./ R min. L		
am pm	oz./ R min. L		
am pm	oz./ R min. L		
am pm	oz./ R min. L		
am pm	oz./ R min. L		
am pm	oz./ R min. L		
am pm	oz./ R min. L		
am pm	oz./ R min. L		

Baby B

Time	Breast/Bottle	Diaper	Meds
am pm	oz./ R min. L		
am pm	oz./ R min. L		
am pm	oz./ R min. L		
am pm	oz./ R min. L		
am pm	oz./ R min. L		
am pm	oz./ R min. L		
am pm	oz./ R min. L		
am pm	oz./ R min. L		

To Do

Naps

start	finish

Notes

Naps

start	finish

Notes

Reminders

twin tracker

TODAY IS:

Baby A

Time		Breast/Bottle	Diaper	Meds
am	pm	oz. / R min. L		
am	pm	oz. / R min. L		
am	pm	oz. / R min. L		
am	pm	oz. / R min. L		
am	pm	oz. / R min. L		
am	pm	oz. / R min. L		
am	pm	oz. / R min. L		
am	pm	oz. / R min. L		

Baby B

Time		Breast/Bottle	Diaper	Meds
am	pm	oz. / R min. L		
am	pm	oz. / R min. L		
am	pm	oz. / R min. L		
am	pm	oz. / R min. L		
am	pm	oz. / R min. L		
am	pm	oz. / R min. L		
am	pm	oz. / R min. L		
am	pm	oz. / R min. L		

To Do

Reminders

Naps

start	finish

Notes

Naps

start	finish

Notes

twin tracker

TODAY IS:

Baby A

Time	Breast/Bottle	Diaper	Meds
am pm	oz./ R min. L		
am pm	oz./ R min. L		
am pm	oz./ R min. L		
am pm	oz./ R min. L		
am pm	oz./ R min. L		
am pm	oz./ R min. L		
am pm	oz./ R min. L		
am pm	oz./ R min. L		

Baby B

Time	Breast/Bottle	Diaper	Meds
am pm	oz./ R min. L		
am pm	oz./ R min. L		
am pm	oz./ R min. L		
am pm	oz./ R min. L		
am pm	oz./ R min. L		
am pm	oz./ R min. L		
am pm	oz./ R min. L		
am pm	oz./ R min. L		

To Do

Naps

start	finish

Notes

Naps

start	finish

Notes

Reminders

twin tracker

TODAY IS:

Baby A

Time	Breast/Bottle	Diaper	Meds
am pm	oz./ R min. L		
am pm	oz./ R min. L		
am pm	oz./ R min. L		
am pm	oz./ R min. L		
am pm	oz./ R min. L		
am pm	oz./ R min. L		
am pm	oz./ R min. L		
am pm	oz./ R min. L		

Baby B

Time	Breast/Bottle	Diaper	Meds
am pm	oz./ R min. L		
am pm	oz./ R min. L		
am pm	oz./ R min. L		
am pm	oz./ R min. L		
am pm	oz./ R min. L		
am pm	oz./ R min. L		
am pm	oz./ R min. L		
am pm	oz./ R min. L		

To Do

Naps

start	finish

Notes

Naps

start	finish

Notes

Reminders

twin tracker

TODAY IS:

Baby A

Time	Breast/Bottle	Diaper	Meds
am pm	oz./ R min. L		
am pm	oz./ R min. L		
am pm	oz./ R min. L		
am pm	oz./ R min. L		
am pm	oz./ R min. L		
am pm	oz./ R min. L		
am pm	oz./ R min. L		
am pm	oz./ R min. L		

Naps

start	finish

Notes
_____
_____
_____
_____
_____

Baby B

Time	Breast/Bottle	Diaper	Meds
am pm	oz./ R min. L		
am pm	oz./ R min. L		
am pm	oz./ R min. L		
am pm	oz./ R min. L		
am pm	oz./ R min. L		
am pm	oz./ R min. L		
am pm	oz./ R min. L		
am pm	oz./ R min. L		

Naps

start	finish

Notes
_____
_____
_____
_____
_____

To Do

Reminders
_____
_____
_____
_____
_____
_____
_____
_____

twin tracker

TODAY IS:

Baby A

Time	Breast/Bottle	Diaper	Meds
am pm	oz./ R min. L		
am pm	oz./ R min. L		
am pm	oz./ R min. L		
am pm	oz./ R min. L		
am pm	oz./ R min. L		
am pm	oz./ R min. L		
am pm	oz./ R min. L		
am pm	oz./ R min. L		

Baby B

Time	Breast/Bottle	Diaper	Meds
am pm	oz./ R min. L		
am pm	oz./ R min. L		
am pm	oz./ R min. L		
am pm	oz./ R min. L		
am pm	oz./ R min. L		
am pm	oz./ R min. L		
am pm	oz./ R min. L		
am pm	oz./ R min. L		

To Do

Naps

start	finish

Notes

Naps

start	finish

Notes

Reminders

twin tracker

TODAY IS:

Baby A

Time	Breast/Bottle	Diaper	Meds
am pm	oz./ R min. L		
am pm	oz./ R min. L		
am pm	oz./ R min. L		
am pm	oz./ R min. L		
am pm	oz./ R min. L		
am pm	oz./ R min. L		
am pm	oz./ R min. L		
am pm	oz./ R min. L		

Naps

start	finish

Notes

_____
_____
_____
_____
_____
_____

Baby B

Time	Breast/Bottle	Diaper	Meds
am pm	oz./ R min. L		
am pm	oz./ R min. L		
am pm	oz./ R min. L		
am pm	oz./ R min. L		
am pm	oz./ R min. L		
am pm	oz./ R min. L		
am pm	oz./ R min. L		
am pm	oz./ R min. L		

Naps

start	finish

Notes

_____
_____
_____
_____
_____
_____

To Do

Reminders

_____
_____
_____
_____
_____
_____
_____
_____

twin tracker

TODAY IS:

Baby A

Time		Breast/Bottle	Diaper	Meds
am pm		oz./ R min. L		
am pm		oz./ R min. L		
am pm		oz./ R min. L		
am pm		oz./ R min. L		
am pm		oz./ R min. L		
am pm		oz./ R min. L		
am pm		oz./ R min. L		
am pm		oz./ R min. L		

Naps

start	finish

Notes

_____
_____
_____
_____
_____

Baby B

Time		Breast/Bottle	Diaper	Meds
am pm		oz./ R min. L		
am pm		oz./ R min. L		
am pm		oz./ R min. L		
am pm		oz./ R min. L		
am pm		oz./ R min. L		
am pm		oz./ R min. L		
am pm		oz./ R min. L		
am pm		oz./ R min. L		

Naps

start	finish

Notes

_____
_____
_____
_____
_____

To Do

Reminders

_____
_____
_____
_____
_____
_____
_____

twin tracker

TODAY IS:

Baby A

Time	Breast/Bottle	Diaper	Meds
am pm	oz./ R min. L		
am pm	oz./ R min. L		
am pm	oz./ R min. L		
am pm	oz./ R min. L		
am pm	oz./ R min. L		
am pm	oz./ R min. L		
am pm	oz./ R min. L		
am pm	oz./ R min. L		

Baby B

Time	Breast/Bottle	Diaper	Meds
am pm	oz./ R min. L		
am pm	oz./ R min. L		
am pm	oz./ R min. L		
am pm	oz./ R min. L		
am pm	oz./ R min. L		
am pm	oz./ R min. L		
am pm	oz./ R min. L		
am pm	oz./ R min. L		

To Do

Naps

start	finish

Notes

Naps

start	finish

Notes

Reminders

twin tracker

TODAY IS:

Baby A

Time		Breast/Bottle	Diaper	Meds
am	pm	oz./ R min. L		
am	pm	oz./ R min. L		
am	pm	oz./ R min. L		
am	pm	oz./ R min. L		
am	pm	oz./ R min. L		
am	pm	oz./ R min. L		
am	pm	oz./ R min. L		
am	pm	oz./ R min. L		

Naps

start	finish

Notes

_____
_____
_____
_____
_____
_____

Baby B

Time		Breast/Bottle	Diaper	Meds
am	pm	oz./ R min. L		
am	pm	oz./ R min. L		
am	pm	oz./ R min. L		
am	pm	oz./ R min. L		
am	pm	oz./ R min. L		
am	pm	oz./ R min. L		
am	pm	oz./ R min. L		
am	pm	oz./ R min. L		

Naps

start	finish

Notes

_____
_____
_____
_____
_____
_____

To Do

Reminders

_____
_____
_____
_____
_____
_____
_____

twin tracker

TODAY IS:

Baby A

Time	Breast/Bottle	Diaper	Meds
am pm	oz./ R min. L		
am pm	oz./ R min. L		
am pm	oz./ R min. L		
am pm	oz./ R min. L		
am pm	oz./ R min. L		
am pm	oz./ R min. L		
am pm	oz./ R min. L		
am pm	oz./ R min. L		

Naps

start	finish

Notes

_____
_____
_____
_____
_____
_____

Baby B

Time	Breast/Bottle	Diaper	Meds
am pm	oz./ R min. L		
am pm	oz./ R min. L		
am pm	oz./ R min. L		
am pm	oz./ R min. L		
am pm	oz./ R min. L		
am pm	oz./ R min. L		
am pm	oz./ R min. L		
am pm	oz./ R min. L		

Naps

start	finish

Notes

_____
_____
_____
_____
_____
_____

To Do

Reminders

_____
_____
_____
_____
_____
_____
_____
_____

twin tracker

TODAY IS:

Baby A

Time	Breast/Bottle	Diaper	Meds
am pm	oz. / R min. L		
am pm	oz. / R min. L		
am pm	oz. / R min. L		
am pm	oz. / R min. L		
am pm	oz. / R min. L		
am pm	oz. / R min. L		
am pm	oz. / R min. L		
am pm	oz. / R min. L		

Baby B

Time	Breast/Bottle	Diaper	Meds
am pm	oz. / R min. L		
am pm	oz. / R min. L		
am pm	oz. / R min. L		
am pm	oz. / R min. L		
am pm	oz. / R min. L		
am pm	oz. / R min. L		
am pm	oz. / R min. L		
am pm	oz. / R min. L		

To Do

Naps

start	finish

Notes

Naps

start	finish

Notes

Reminders

twin tracker

TODAY IS:

Baby A

Time		Breast/ Bottle		Diaper	Meds
am	pm	oz./ min.	R L		
am	pm	oz./ min.	R L		
am	pm	oz./ min.	R L		
am	pm	oz./ min.	R L		
am	pm	oz./ min.	R L		
am	pm	oz./ min.	R L		
am	pm	oz./ min.	R L		
am	pm	oz./ min.	R L		

Naps

start	finish

Notes

_____
_____
_____
_____
_____

Baby B

Time		Breast/ Bottle		Diaper	Meds
am	pm	oz./ min.	R L		
am	pm	oz./ min.	R L		
am	pm	oz./ min.	R L		
am	pm	oz./ min.	R L		
am	pm	oz./ min.	R L		
am	pm	oz./ min.	R L		
am	pm	oz./ min.	R L		
am	pm	oz./ min.	R L		

Naps

start	finish

Notes

_____
_____
_____
_____
_____

To Do

Reminders

_____
_____
_____
_____
_____
_____
_____

twin tracker

TODAY IS:

Baby A

Time	Breast/Bottle	Diaper	Meds
am pm	oz./R min. L		
am pm	oz./R min. L		
am pm	oz./R min. L		
am pm	oz./R min. L		
am pm	oz./R min. L		
am pm	oz./R min. L		
am pm	oz./R min. L		
am pm	oz./R min. L		

Baby B

Time	Breast/Bottle	Diaper	Meds
am pm	oz./R min. L		
am pm	oz./R min. L		
am pm	oz./R min. L		
am pm	oz./R min. L		
am pm	oz./R min. L		
am pm	oz./R min. L		
am pm	oz./R min. L		
am pm	oz./R min. L		

To Do

Naps

start	finish

Notes

Naps

start	finish

Notes

Reminders

twin tracker

TODAY IS:

Baby A

Time	Breast/Bottle	Diaper	Meds
am pm	oz./ R min. L		
am pm	oz./ R min. L		
am pm	oz./ R min. L		
am pm	oz./ R min. L		
am pm	oz./ R min. L		
am pm	oz./ R min. L		
am pm	oz./ R min. L		
am pm	oz./ R min. L		

Naps

start	finish

Notes

_____
_____
_____
_____
_____
_____

Baby B

Time	Breast/Bottle	Diaper	Meds
am pm	oz./ R min. L		
am pm	oz./ R min. L		
am pm	oz./ R min. L		
am pm	oz./ R min. L		
am pm	oz./ R min. L		
am pm	oz./ R min. L		
am pm	oz./ R min. L		
am pm	oz./ R min. L		

Naps

start	finish

Notes

_____
_____
_____
_____
_____
_____

To Do

Reminders

_____
_____
_____
_____
_____
_____
_____

twin tracker

TODAY IS:

Baby A

Time	Breast/Bottle	Diaper	Meds
am pm	oz./ R min. L		
am pm	oz./ R min. L		
am pm	oz./ R min. L		
am pm	oz./ R min. L		
am pm	oz./ R min. L		
am pm	oz./ R min. L		
am pm	oz./ R min. L		
am pm	oz./ R min. L		

Baby B

Time	Breast/Bottle	Diaper	Meds
am pm	oz./ R min. L		
am pm	oz./ R min. L		
am pm	oz./ R min. L		
am pm	oz./ R min. L		
am pm	oz./ R min. L		
am pm	oz./ R min. L		
am pm	oz./ R min. L		
am pm	oz./ R min. L		

To Do

Naps

start	finish

Notes

Naps

start	finish

Notes

Reminders

twin tracker

TODAY IS:

Baby A

Time		Breast/Bottle	Diaper	Meds
am pm		oz./ R min. L		
am pm		oz./ R min. L		
am pm		oz./ R min. L		
am pm		oz./ R min. L		
am pm		oz./ R min. L		
am pm		oz./ R min. L		
am pm		oz./ R min. L		
am pm		oz./ R min. L		

Naps

start	finish

Notes

_____
_____
_____
_____
_____
_____

Baby B

Time		Breast/Bottle	Diaper	Meds
am pm		oz./ R min. L		
am pm		oz./ R min. L		
am pm		oz./ R min. L		
am pm		oz./ R min. L		
am pm		oz./ R min. L		
am pm		oz./ R min. L		
am pm		oz./ R min. L		
am pm		oz./ R min. L		

Naps

start	finish

Notes

_____
_____
_____
_____
_____
_____

To Do

Reminders

_____
_____
_____
_____
_____
_____
_____
_____

twin tracker

TODAY IS:

Baby A

Time		Breast/ Bottle	Diaper	Meds
am pm		oz./ R min. L		
am pm		oz./ R min. L		
am pm		oz./ R min. L		
am pm		oz./ R min. L		
am pm		oz./ R min. L		
am pm		oz./ R min. L		
am pm		oz./ R min. L		
am pm		oz./ R min. L		

Baby B

Time		Breast/ Bottle	Diaper	Meds
am pm		oz./ R min. L		
am pm		oz./ R min. L		
am pm		oz./ R min. L		
am pm		oz./ R min. L		
am pm		oz./ R min. L		
am pm		oz./ R min. L		
am pm		oz./ R min. L		
am pm		oz./ R min. L		

To Do

Naps

start	finish

Notes

_____
_____
_____
_____
_____

Naps

start	finish

Notes

_____
_____
_____
_____
_____

Reminders

_____
_____
_____
_____
_____
_____
_____
_____

twin tracker

TODAY IS:

Baby A

Time	Breast/Bottle	Diaper	Meds
am pm	oz./ R min. L		
am pm	oz./ R min. L		
am pm	oz./ R min. L		
am pm	oz./ R min. L		
am pm	oz./ R min. L		
am pm	oz./ R min. L		
am pm	oz./ R min. L		
am pm	oz./ R min. L		

Baby B

Time	Breast/Bottle	Diaper	Meds
am pm	oz./ R min. L		
am pm	oz./ R min. L		
am pm	oz./ R min. L		
am pm	oz./ R min. L		
am pm	oz./ R min. L		
am pm	oz./ R min. L		
am pm	oz./ R min. L		
am pm	oz./ R min. L		

To Do

Naps

start	finish

Notes

_____
_____
_____
_____
_____
_____

Naps

start	finish

Notes

_____
_____
_____
_____
_____
_____

Reminders

_____
_____
_____
_____
_____
_____
_____

twin tracker

TODAY IS:

Baby A

Time	Breast/Bottle	Diaper	Meds
am pm	oz./ R min. L		
am pm	oz./ R min. L		
am pm	oz./ R min. L		
am pm	oz./ R min. L		
am pm	oz./ R min. L		
am pm	oz./ R min. L		
am pm	oz./ R min. L		
am pm	oz./ R min. L		

Baby B

Time	Breast/Bottle	Diaper	Meds
am pm	oz./ R min. L		
am pm	oz./ R min. L		
am pm	oz./ R min. L		
am pm	oz./ R min. L		
am pm	oz./ R min. L		
am pm	oz./ R min. L		
am pm	oz./ R min. L		
am pm	oz./ R min. L		

To Do

Naps

start	finish

Notes

Naps

start	finish

Notes

Reminders

twin tracker

TODAY IS:

Baby A

Time	Breast/Bottle	Diaper	Meds
am pm	oz./ min. R L		
am pm	oz./ min. R L		
am pm	oz./ min. R L		
am pm	oz./ min. R L		
am pm	oz./ min. R L		
am pm	oz./ min. R L		
am pm	oz./ min. R L		
am pm	oz./ min. R L		

Baby B

Time	Breast/Bottle	Diaper	Meds
am pm	oz./ min. R L		
am pm	oz./ min. R L		
am pm	oz./ min. R L		
am pm	oz./ min. R L		
am pm	oz./ min. R L		
am pm	oz./ min. R L		
am pm	oz./ min. R L		
am pm	oz./ min. R L		

To Do

Naps

start	finish

Notes

Naps

start	finish

Notes

Reminders

twin tracker

TODAY IS:

Baby A

Time	Breast/Bottle	Diaper	Meds
am pm	oz./ R min. L		
am pm	oz./ R min. L		
am pm	oz./ R min. L		
am pm	oz./ R min. L		
am pm	oz./ R min. L		
am pm	oz./ R min. L		
am pm	oz./ R min. L		
am pm	oz./ R min. L		

Baby B

Time	Breast/Bottle	Diaper	Meds
am pm	oz./ R min. L		
am pm	oz./ R min. L		
am pm	oz./ R min. L		
am pm	oz./ R min. L		
am pm	oz./ R min. L		
am pm	oz./ R min. L		
am pm	oz./ R min. L		
am pm	oz./ R min. L		

To Do

Naps

start	finish

Notes

Naps

start	finish

Notes

Reminders

twin tracker

TODAY IS:

Baby A

Time	Breast/Bottle	Diaper	Meds
am pm	oz./ R min. L		
am pm	oz./ R min. L		
am pm	oz./ R min. L		
am pm	oz./ R min. L		
am pm	oz./ R min. L		
am pm	oz./ R min. L		
am pm	oz./ R min. L		
am pm	oz./ R min. L		

Naps

start	finish

Notes

_____
_____
_____
_____
_____
_____

Baby B

Time	Breast/Bottle	Diaper	Meds
am pm	oz./ R min. L		
am pm	oz./ R min. L		
am pm	oz./ R min. L		
am pm	oz./ R min. L		
am pm	oz./ R min. L		
am pm	oz./ R min. L		
am pm	oz./ R min. L		
am pm	oz./ R min. L		

Naps

start	finish

Notes

_____
_____
_____
_____
_____
_____

To Do

Reminders

_____
_____
_____
_____
_____
_____
_____
_____

twin tracker

TODAY IS:

Baby A

Time	Breast/Bottle	Diaper	Meds
am pm	oz./ R min. L		
am pm	oz./ R min. L		
am pm	oz./ R min. L		
am pm	oz./ R min. L		
am pm	oz./ R min. L		
am pm	oz./ R min. L		
am pm	oz./ R min. L		
am pm	oz./ R min. L		

Baby B

Time	Breast/Bottle	Diaper	Meds
am pm	oz./ R min. L		
am pm	oz./ R min. L		
am pm	oz./ R min. L		
am pm	oz./ R min. L		
am pm	oz./ R min. L		
am pm	oz./ R min. L		
am pm	oz./ R min. L		
am pm	oz./ R min. L		

To Do

Naps

start	finish

Notes

Naps

start	finish

Notes

Reminders

twin tracker

TODAY IS:

Baby A

Time	Breast/Bottle	Diaper	Meds
am pm	oz./ R min. L		
am pm	oz./ R min. L		
am pm	oz./ R min. L		
am pm	oz./ R min. L		
am pm	oz./ R min. L		
am pm	oz./ R min. L		
am pm	oz./ R min. L		
am pm	oz./ R min. L		

Baby B

Time	Breast/Bottle	Diaper	Meds
am pm	oz./ R min. L		
am pm	oz./ R min. L		
am pm	oz./ R min. L		
am pm	oz./ R min. L		
am pm	oz./ R min. L		
am pm	oz./ R min. L		
am pm	oz./ R min. L		
am pm	oz./ R min. L		

To Do

Naps

start	finish

Notes

_____
_____
_____
_____
_____
_____
_____

Naps

start	finish

Notes

_____
_____
_____
_____
_____
_____
_____

Reminders

_____
_____
_____
_____
_____
_____
_____
_____

twin tracker

TODO IS:

Baby A

Time	Breast/Bottle	Diaper	Meds
am pm	oz./ R min. L		
am pm	oz./ R min. L		
am pm	oz./ R min. L		
am pm	oz./ R min. L		
am pm	oz./ R min. L		
am pm	oz./ R min. L		
am pm	oz./ R min. L		
am pm	oz./ R min. L		

Naps

start	finish

Notes

_____
_____
_____
_____
_____

Baby B

Time	Breast/Bottle	Diaper	Meds
am pm	oz./ R min. L		
am pm	oz./ R min. L		
am pm	oz./ R min. L		
am pm	oz./ R min. L		
am pm	oz./ R min. L		
am pm	oz./ R min. L		
am pm	oz./ R min. L		
am pm	oz./ R min. L		

Naps

start	finish

Notes

_____
_____
_____
_____
_____

To Do

Reminders

_____
_____
_____
_____
_____
_____

twin tracker

TODAY IS:

Baby A

Time	Breast/Bottle	Diaper	Meds
am pm	oz./ R min. L		
am pm	oz./ R min. L		
am pm	oz./ R min. L		
am pm	oz./ R min. L		
am pm	oz./ R min. L		
am pm	oz./ R min. L		
am pm	oz./ R min. L		
am pm	oz./ R min. L		

Baby B

Time	Breast/Bottle	Diaper	Meds
am pm	oz./ R min. L		
am pm	oz./ R min. L		
am pm	oz./ R min. L		
am pm	oz./ R min. L		
am pm	oz./ R min. L		
am pm	oz./ R min. L		
am pm	oz./ R min. L		
am pm	oz./ R min. L		

To Do

Naps

start	finish

Notes

Naps

start	finish

Notes

Reminders

twin tracker

TODAY IS:

Baby A

Time	Breast/Bottle	Diaper	Meds
am pm	oz./ R min. L		
am pm	oz./ R min. L		
am pm	oz./ R min. L		
am pm	oz./ R min. L		
am pm	oz./ R min. L		
am pm	oz./ R min. L		
am pm	oz./ R min. L		
am pm	oz./ R min. L		

Baby B

Time	Breast/Bottle	Diaper	Meds
am pm	oz./ R min. L		
am pm	oz./ R min. L		
am pm	oz./ R min. L		
am pm	oz./ R min. L		
am pm	oz./ R min. L		
am pm	oz./ R min. L		
am pm	oz./ R min. L		
am pm	oz./ R min. L		

To Do

Naps

start	finish

Notes

Naps

start	finish

Notes

Reminders

twin tracker

TODAY IS:

Baby A

Time	Breast/Bottle	Diaper	Meds
am pm	oz./ R min. L		
am pm	oz./ R min. L		
am pm	oz./ R min. L		
am pm	oz./ R min. L		
am pm	oz./ R min. L		
am pm	oz./ R min. L		
am pm	oz./ R min. L		
am pm	oz./ R min. L		

Baby B

Time	Breast/Bottle	Diaper	Meds
am pm	oz./ R min. L		
am pm	oz./ R min. L		
am pm	oz./ R min. L		
am pm	oz./ R min. L		
am pm	oz./ R min. L		
am pm	oz./ R min. L		
am pm	oz./ R min. L		
am pm	oz./ R min. L		

To Do

Naps

start	finish	Notes

Naps

start	finish	Notes

Reminders

twin tracker

TODAY IS:

Baby A

Time	Breast/Bottle	Diaper	Meds
am pm	oz./ R min. L		
am pm	oz./ R min. L		
am pm	oz./ R min. L		
am pm	oz./ R min. L		
am pm	oz./ R min. L		
am pm	oz./ R min. L		
am pm	oz./ R min. L		
am pm	oz./ R min. L		

Naps

start	finish

Notes

_____
_____
_____
_____
_____
_____

Baby B

Time	Breast/Bottle	Diaper	Meds
am pm	oz./ R min. L		
am pm	oz./ R min. L		
am pm	oz./ R min. L		
am pm	oz./ R min. L		
am pm	oz./ R min. L		
am pm	oz./ R min. L		
am pm	oz./ R min. L		
am pm	oz./ R min. L		

Naps

start	finish

Notes

_____
_____
_____
_____
_____
_____

To Do

Reminders

twin tracker

TODAY IS:

Baby A

Time	Breast/Bottle	Diaper	Meds
am pm	oz./ R min. L		
am pm	oz./ R min. L		
am pm	oz./ R min. L		
am pm	oz./ R min. L		
am pm	oz./ R min. L		
am pm	oz./ R min. L		
am pm	oz./ R min. L		
am pm	oz./ R min. L		

Baby B

Time	Breast/Bottle	Diaper	Meds
am pm	oz./ R min. L		
am pm	oz./ R min. L		
am pm	oz./ R min. L		
am pm	oz./ R min. L		
am pm	oz./ R min. L		
am pm	oz./ R min. L		
am pm	oz./ R min. L		
am pm	oz./ R min. L		

To Do

Naps

start	finish	Notes

Naps

start	finish	Notes

Reminders

twin tracker

TODAY IS:

Baby A

Time	Breast/Bottle	Diaper	Meds
am pm	oz./ R min. L		
am pm	oz./ R min. L		
am pm	oz./ R min. L		
am pm	oz./ R min. L		
am pm	oz./ R min. L		
am pm	oz./ R min. L		
am pm	oz./ R min. L		
am pm	oz./ R min. L		

Baby B

Time	Breast/Bottle	Diaper	Meds
am pm	oz./ R min. L		
am pm	oz./ R min. L		
am pm	oz./ R min. L		
am pm	oz./ R min. L		
am pm	oz./ R min. L		
am pm	oz./ R min. L		
am pm	oz./ R min. L		
am pm	oz./ R min. L		

To Do

Naps

start	finish

Notes

Naps

start	finish

Notes

Reminders

twin tracker

TODAY IS:

Baby A

Time	Breast/Bottle	Diaper	Meds
am pm	oz./ R min. L		
am pm	oz./ R min. L		
am pm	oz./ R min. L		
am pm	oz./ R min. L		
am pm	oz./ R min. L		
am pm	oz./ R min. L		
am pm	oz./ R min. L		
am pm	oz./ R min. L		

Naps

start	finish

Notes

_____
_____
_____
_____
_____
_____

Baby B

Time	Breast/Bottle	Diaper	Meds
am pm	oz./ R min. L		
am pm	oz./ R min. L		
am pm	oz./ R min. L		
am pm	oz./ R min. L		
am pm	oz./ R min. L		
am pm	oz./ R min. L		
am pm	oz./ R min. L		
am pm	oz./ R min. L		

Naps

start	finish

Notes

_____
_____
_____
_____
_____
_____

To Do

Reminders

_____
_____
_____
_____
_____
_____
_____
_____

twin tracker

TODAY IS: